THE RENAISSANCE TAROT

THE RENAISSANCE TAROT

LEGENDS OF THE PAST NOW REVEAL THE FUTURE

JANE LYLE

CARDS ILLUSTRATED BY HELEN JONES

A Fireside Book
Published by Simon & Schuster

For all those with a place in my heart

F FIRESIDE
Rockefeller Center
1230 Avenue of the Americas
New York, NY 10020

Text copyright © 1998 by Jane Lyle
Card illustrations copyright © 1998 by Helen Jones
Card photography copyright © 1998 by Stephen Marwood
This edition copyright © 1998 by Eddison Sadd Editions

All rights reserved, including the right of reproduction in whole or in part in any form.

The right of Jane Lyle to be identified as the author of this work has been asserted by her in accordance with the Copyright, Designs and Patents Act 1988.

First published in Great Britain by Judy Piatkus (Publishers) Ltd.
Published by arrangement with Eddison Sadd Editions Limited.

FIRESIDE and colophon are registered trademarks of Simon & Schuster Inc.

1 3 5 7 9 10 8 6 4 2

Library of Congress Cataloging-in-Publication Data is available.

ISBN 0-684-85490-2

AN EDDISON•SADD EDITION
Edited, designed and produced by
Eddison Sadd Editions Limited
St Chad's House, 148 King's Cross Road
London WC1X 9DH

Phototypeset in Carmina BT using QuarkXPress on Apple Macintosh
Origination by Atlas Mediacom (S) Pte Ltd, Singapore
Printed in China by L. Rex Printing Company

CONTENTS

INTRODUCTION 6

Part One THE MAJOR ARCANA 8

The Pairs 9

0	THE FOOL	12	XI	STRENGTH	56
I	THE MAGICIAN	16	XII	THE HANGED MAN	60
II	THE HIGH PRIESTESS	20	XIII	DEATH	64
III	THE EMPRESS	24	XIV	TEMPERANCE	68
IV	THE EMPEROR	28	XV	THE DEVIL	72
V	THE HIEROPHANT	32	XVI	THE TOWER	76
VI	THE LOVERS	36	XVII	THE STAR	80
VII	THE CHARIOT	40	XVIII	THE MOON	84
VIII	JUSTICE	44	XIX	THE SUN	88
IX	THE HERMIT	48	XX	JUDGEMENT	92
X	THE WHEEL OF FORTUNE	52	XXI	THE WORLD	96

Part Two THE MINOR ARCANA 100

Mythic Origins 100
The Four Elements and the Minor Arcana 102
Numerology and the Minor Arcana 103

THE SUIT OF WANDS	104	THE SUIT OF SWORDS	138
THE SUIT OF PENTACLES	121	THE SUIT OF CUPS	155

Part Three HOW TO USE THE RENAISSANCE TAROT 172

Tarot Reading – A Basic Guide 172
Timing 176

TRADITIONAL LAYOUTS 178

The Horseshoe Spread	178	The Celtic Cross	184
The Romany Spread	180	Sample Readings	186
The Horoscope Spread	182		

Appendix: Symbols 190
Bibliography and Further Reading 191
About the Author 191
About the Artist 191
Acknowledgements 192

INTRODUCTION

The tarot exerts a mysterious allure. Its accessible history is a tantalizing blend of slender facts and romantic speculation, while its symbols continue to have a powerful impact on everyone who sees them. Even its name defies classification, because no one knows for certain what the word 'tarot' actually means, or which language it might spring from.

We know that the tarot first appeared in Europe during the late fourteenth century – it did not exist before then. The earliest cards, of which seventeen remain, date from 1392. Thirty years later, Bonifacio Bembo, an Italian artist, created a deck for the powerful Visconti family. This deck is the oldest complete set of tarot cards to survive, placing the tarot and its images against the backdrop of the Renaissance, which was one of the most culturally exciting periods in history.

The Dark Ages preceded the medieval period. The Middle Ages were named by the Renaissance thinkers to distinguish them from their own period of history, in a somewhat derogatory fashion. However, much of the symbolism and knowledge which bloomed during the Renaissance owes its source to the Crusades, and the opening up of the communication with the Arab world and what became the vast empires of Byzantium. The word 'renaissance' means 'rebirth'. During this era – which represents a shifting time zone including the High Renaissance, and shading into the Baroque period – philosophy, art, science and religion underwent an astonishing regeneration. Classical Greek culture was rediscovered, and oriental esoteric teachings, including astrology and alchemy, began to filter into Europe through the learned Arab scholars of Spain and North Africa, and from the influence of the exotic Byzantine Empire, whose power emanated from Constantinople, now Istanbul. A heady mixture of knowledge, veiled and hidden throughout the Dark Ages and the medieval period, invigorated the finest minds of Italy and western Europe. The tarot's multifarious characters and symbols act out their elusive dramas upon this glittering stage.

The tarot, and in particular the Major Arcana's twenty-two trump cards, has often been referred to as a book. Antoine Court de Gébelin (1728–84) was a French philosopher who rediscovered the tarot, believing it to be an ancient Egyptian book of secret spiritual teachings. That it is a visual record of secret doctrines seems highly likely. It is impossible not to wonder about the deeper significance of the High Priestess, or Papess, for example.

Medieval rumours about a

female pope were widespread, but the very idea of a feminine priestess was heretical and deeply rooted in pagan belief. Women with spiritual powers were classified as witches or placed in convents, tucked safely away from the world of men. However, alchemists relied upon women's assistance in their work – the figure of the 'mystic sister' appears in all the great alchemical works, as does the idea of the symbolic wedding of male and female energies. The planetary symbols of the tarot – the Sun, Moon and Star – link it to astrology, while the apocalyptic image of the Tower, or House of God, suggests the destruction of the prevailing establishment. Making a visual record of these ideas would have been one way to disseminate such dangerous information during a time when heretics were burned at the stake. This was an era when people had a passion for allegory, metaphor, visual mysteries and puzzles. They designed gardens that led the visitor through re-creations of classical mythology, they included obscure symbolism in their paintings and even in their architecture. They were in many ways more visually sophisticated than ourselves, crafting their surroundings from raw materials, rather than relying on television or film to supply sights and scenes.

Visual prompts as keys to spiritual states of mind were also a favourite Renaissance device. The art of memory, as it was known, involved intense meditation upon spiritually inspired images, leading to enlightened understanding of the pictures involved. By holding the image in the mind, knowledge far beyond what could be communicated orally or in writing could be obtained and absorbed. Presenting a spiritual progression, from ignorance to enlightened wisdom, as a series of pictures perfectly fits the philosophical practices of the time.

At the deepest levels, the tarot's images defy analysis. No sooner is one category created for them than another appears. This, in part, is because the images themselves draw upon the rich brew of Gnosticism, classical Greek philosophy, alchemy, heretical belief and pagan myth. It is also because the symbols are archetypal, reflecting characters in fairytales and dreams.

Since the very first tarot cards appeared during the Renaissance, this seemed an appropriate place to begin the process of creating a brand-new deck that would reveal some of the intricate and ancient philosophies behind its intriguing symbolism. By using fresh and sometimes surprising imagery we hope to sweep away the last vestiges of superstition and ignorance that still cling to the tarot, and present a vibrant symbolic system for clarifying hopes, fears, wishes and heartfelt dreams. As Albert Einstein wrote: 'Imagination is more important than knowledge.' May you enjoy the dreams presented herein.

Part One

THE MAJOR ARCANA

THE MAJOR ARCANA, OR GREATER SECRETS, IS A POTENT COLLECTION OF SYMBOLS. LIKE THE CAST OF CHARACTERS FROM SOME EXOTIC DREAM, THEY TROOP PAST IN A PARADE LED BY THE LIGHT-HEARTED FOOL – EACH REVEALING GLIMPSES OF WISDOM, EACH CONCEALING THE HEART OF THEIR OWN MYSTERIES. AND, ONCE STUDIED IN ANY DEPTH, IT IS CLEAR THAT THEY REPRESENT A SPIRITUAL QUEST, A JOURNEY OF INITIATION.

Such adventures are found in fairytales, myths, legends and within the teachings of ancient mystery religions. Elements are found in contemporary personal growth movements, psychoanalysis, astrology, positive thinking and even complementary medicine. Generally, however, these movements lack the seductive fascination of traditional teachings, for in attempting to deconstruct myth and make magic and mystery accessible they have overlooked the intense, wordless power of symbols. Those who created the Major Arcana understood this very well. In a largely illiterate world, pictures were worth infinitely more than words. The complex stories that the pictures of the tarot tell are, in any event, more suited to intuitive understanding than intellectual reasoning.

The journey of initiation revealed here is a cyclical one. The Wheel of Fortune turns forever at its halfway point, the World is both last trump and new turning point – ushering in an untrodden curve in the eternal spiral of life, death and rebirth.

There are twenty-two images, forming eleven pairs. The first eleven cards represent the outer world, the first stages, tests, challenges and rewards. Their partners, following on after the Wheel of Fortune (X), represent the second stage of initiation, deeper knowledge and profound inner experiences. For the purposes of divination, all cards may indicate circumstances in the inner worlds or represent actual events in the outer world. Often, these are simultaneous – inner changes affect the tangible world, outer events give rise to contemplation, analysis and change. The pairs are connected with the structure of the Major Arcana as a whole entity, a description of the inner and outer worlds it mirrors. Should a pair appear in a reading, it would indicate the emergence of a strong theme, described by the particular pair, in the reading. The rest of the reading will strengthen or weaken this theme, according to the nature of the cards.

The initiatory journey of the tarot trumps reflects life itself – a spiritual challenge can appear in the form of a job, relationship, child or friendship, just as these everyday matters can bring blessings and a sense of rebirth. Where spirit and matter are one, as the philosophy behind the tarot teaches, divisions eventually become meaningless.

For *The Renaissance Tarot* we have included subtle design links between these pairs, to highlight their mysterious partnership and to enhance your sense of the Major Arcana as a complete entity, rather than a jumbled series of images. Here is a brief outline of their story, their position on the Wheel of Infinity, and their relevance to one another.

The Pairs

0 The Fool • XX Judgement
The innocent Fool, setting out untried and untested by life, eventually acquires wisdom and soulful qualities by experiencing all the stages represented by the cards between 0 and XX.

I The Magician • XIX The Sun
The Magician begins to explore and experiment with the worlds he can see, and also with the unseen realms. He can travel to the underworld, or unconscious depths, and reach the heavenly heights and light

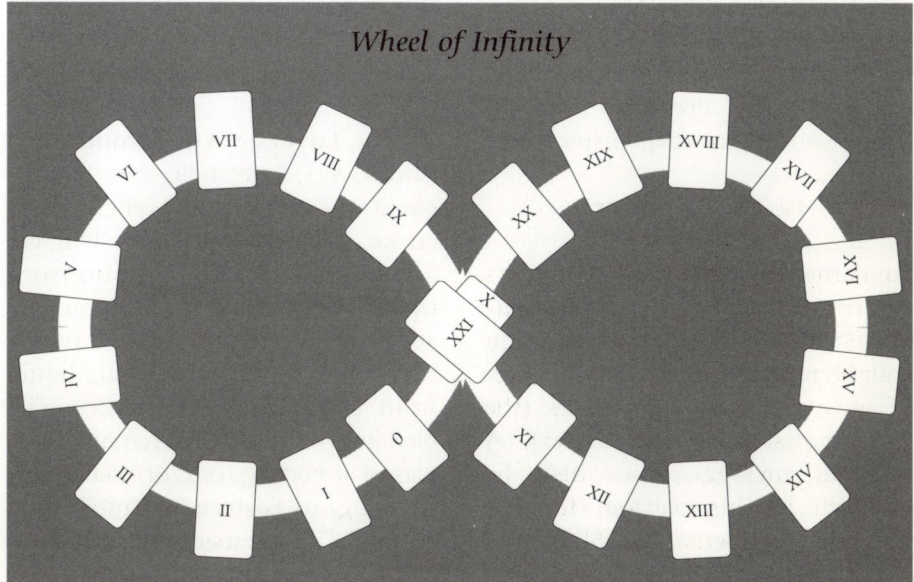
Wheel of Infinity

of awareness symbolized by the Sun. Magic, alchemy, astrology and the development of intricate symbolism flourished during the Renaissance.

II The High Priestess
XVIII The Moon

The veiled goddess is paired with her unearthly kingdom, the lunar world of the Moon. She opens the gates of feminine mystery to the seeking Fool.

III The Empress • XVII The Star

Two faces of the goddess are now revealed. As the Empress, she is the fertile mother; as the Star, she is the naked goddess who reveals herself as inspiration, guidance and hope. Feminine deities were largely viewed with suspicion by the established medieval Church. Nonetheless, this period saw the flowering of an enduring cult of the Virgin Mary. During the Renaissance, goddesses were represented by artists and sculptors who drew on classical pagan sources for their inspiration.

IV The Emperor
XVI The Tower

Fundamentally, this pair represents the transformation of the masculine principle (the Emperor) through enlightenment, and the destruction of outworn values or beliefs (the lightning striking the Tower). A political message may also be intended in this pairing, for the Emperor represents the State and the Tower signifies the downfall of what was, at the time, the Holy Roman Empire. This message was based on the beliefs and hopes of the Gnostics, Cathars and other heretical religious groups of the medieval and Renaissance period.

V The Hierophant
XV The Devil

Again, a veiled political message about the corrupt nature and worldly powers of medieval clergy may be read into this pair of traditional adversaries. However, this combination also symbolizes the eternal pairing of the forces of bright reason (the Hierophant/Pope) with the powers of instinct (the Devil). Reason is lifeless and even misleading when divorced from instinct, while instinct and intuition are refined and shaped by reason and structure. In Greek mythology this is represented by the pairing of Apollo, god of reason, with Dionysus, god of instinctual anarchy.

VI The Lovers • XIV Temperance

The Lovers, one male, one female, blend their individual energies to create a balanced whole. Temperance is derived from the Latin word *temperare*, meaning 'to mix, moderate or bring into harmony', which is why she is shown pouring liquid from one vessel to another. The blending of male and female energies is a cornerstone of alchemical teaching, of Eastern Tantra, of traditional Chinese medicine and many spiritual philosophies.

THE PAIRS

VII The Chariot • XIII Death

Here, the Fool is confronted by time, death and progress. The Chariot proceeds along the symbolic road of time, night and day, victory and defeat. Part of this journey is a meeting with Death, which comes in many forms throughout life – all partings, endings and conclusions are forms of death. The message of this pair is that there can be no progress, or indeed true life, without death – since this is always followed by some form of rebirth. This pair represents the need for us to surrender, to let go and move forward in life.

VIII Justice
XII The Hanged Man

This pair has a similar feeling to the Hierophant and the Devil, for it combines cool logic (Justice) with visionary dreams and intuitive promptings (the Hanged Man). However, this pair represent a more conscious blending of these two qualities and teach that balance is needed when exploring the upside-down world of the Hanged Man.

IX The Hermit • XI Strength

These two cards represent the gift of spiritual contemplation, strengthened by the power of love and faith. Everything is reduced to its essence prior to transformation – a period of withdrawal and introspection (the Hermit) is followed by joyful creativity and triumph (Strength). Both withdrawal and creativity are needed at different times in life.

X The Wheel of Fortune
XXI The World

This pair represent the greater and lesser cycles of change and development in life. Each opens a new stage, with its own adventures, pitfalls and choices. Each is eternal, representing fate, karma, destiny and the results of life choices.

For *The Renaissance Tarot* we have chosen to use modern astrological rulerships, which include Uranus, Neptune and Pluto, for the cards. These three planets were unknown to ancient astrologers. However, this deck was conceived in the true spirit of renaissance, that is, rebirth. Contemporary astrological knowledge is sophisticated, and an understanding of these modern planetary symbols serves to add depth to the interpretation of each image.

It is in the same spirit that we have altered some of the traditional designs of the tarot, using mythical creatures to enhance the cards' meanings and create an atmosphere of mystery. *The Renaissance Tarot* is very much a deck for our times, inspired by the tarot's own origins, and reinvented in the hopes of a new renaissance.

THE MAJOR ARCANA

— 0 —
THE FOOL

RULING PLANET
Uranus

KEYWORDS
UPRIGHT: Adventure • Change • Energy
REVERSED: Instability • Ambiguity

BUTTERFLIES
denote the Fool's quest for wisdom and the knowledge that springs from the soul itself

WHITE ROSES
symbolize innocence, purity and renewal

BLACK AND SILVER
signify the active and passive energies that the Fool must combine

URANUS
is the planet of change and revolution, and challenges stale convention

LUTE
links the Fool with Orpheus, who also had to descend to the underworld in order to transform himself

LITTLE DOG
keeps the Fool on the right path and gives him fidelity, watchfulness, devotion and duality

Symbolism of the Card

THE ELUSIVE, DANCING FIGURE OF THE FOOL INTRODUCES THE
TWENTY-TWO TRUMPS OF THE MAJOR ARCANA.

His number is zero, which is not really a number at all. Zero signifies the circular path of the tarot's own journey of learning and experience, and that of every life that is lived to the full.

This androgynous figure is dressed in a **black and silver** costume, signifying his dual nature and the active and passive energies that must be combined to achieve wholeness. Black symbolizes the unknown, the earth, night and the shadows that the Fool will encounter on the initiatory journey. Silver signifies spirit, potential enlightenment and the illuminating insights that the Fool will experience.

Like the troubadours and roving musicians of medieval and Renaissance Europe, the Fool carries a *lute*. Music signifies harmony and change; the lute itself is connected with Orpheus, who entered the underworld and returned with the spiritual revelations that formed the basis of Orphism, a flourishing mystery religion. The Fool, like Orpheus, must make the descent into the underworld and re-emerge, changed and refined by the experience.

The **white roses** that frame the figure are symbols of innocence, purity and renewal. Alchemists used the rose as a symbol of wisdom and of the process of alchemy.

The innocent Fool stands on the brink of a spiritual journey in which his or her untapped wisdom will be revealed, just as the ancient alchemists sought to reveal precious gold, or the elixir of life, by their intricate efforts.

The **butterflies** are universal soul symbols, the end result of a process of transformation from caterpillar to beautiful winged creature. They represent the spirit within every living being, and here also denote the Fool's quest for wisdom and for the knowledge that springs from the soul itself.

A **little dog** accompanies the Fool on this quest. It possesses several important qualities – faithfulness, watchfulness, devotion and also duality – for within every domesticated dog is the distant race memory of its wild ancestors. It is here to keep the Fool on the right path, and is a companion of the virgin goddesses such as wild Greek Artemis, of messenger gods such as Hermes, and of underworld deities.

The astrological symbols of the planet **Uranus** have been included on the upper corners of this card. Uranus is the planet of revolution and change, and always challenges stale convention wherever this appears to be stifling life, growth, change and vitality.

The Spirit of Anarchy

The Fool, or Jester, was a familiar figure throughout the medieval and Renaissance period. He appears in Shakespeare, in paintings, poetry and stories. He is innocent, knowing, quick-witted, comical, tragic and, above all, free from the constraints of normal society. He represents the forces of chaos, energy yet to be educated and shaped.

In the traditional royal court, the jester could do or say the most irreverent things. The Fool of the tarot contains all these meanings and, as the card numbered zero, signifies the beginnings and endings of all cycles. It seems fitting that this is the only Major Arcana figure to appear in the regular pack of playing cards. Risk-taking, gambling, the capriciousness of luck and fortune – all these are associated with card games, and also with the Fool.

The Fool also has strong links with the troubadours, or wandering minstrels, who travelled around Europe carrying their pagan poetry with them. These men and women praised the power of love, and often personified it as a goddess. Aspects of love, such as jealousy, were also personified as semi-divine figures. Some scholars believe that the old gods and goddesses of pagan Europe were revived by the Courtly Love movement, whose poets and singers were the troubadours. This movement glorified women, and believed in the blending of spiritual and sexual energies in a way that is reminiscent of oriental Tantric teachings on sexuality. They promoted the philosophy that the bliss of both body and soul combined creates a complete expression of spiritual grace.

Like the trickster gods of old, troubadours knew the power of words, the charm of poetry and the enchanting qualities of music and song. In this way, they were able to spread these subversive ideas, praising pleasure and the mystical secrets of love, wherever they went. As seditious figures, like the Fool, they were mistrusted by the established Church, whose fear of women was based on the need to eradicate thousands of years of goddess worship. The elimination and suppression of feminine deities was a central motif of the Christian Church's development; only mystics and pagans kept alive the idea of the divine feminine. This same theme may be seen within Judaism and Islam, where the spiritual power of the divine feminine was only acknowledged freely within the mystical cults (the Jewish cabbala and the Islamic Sufi movement). Since the tarot presents all aspects of the goddess – figures who teach the Fool and guide him through his initiation – it is not surprising that it was condemned at the time of its creation and in all the centuries that followed.

THE FOOL

Upright Meaning

The fluid energy of the Fool signifies a new beginning. When the Fool appears, you are on the threshold of a journey. It may be mental, physical, spiritual or emotional but, whatever form it takes, your preconceived ideas and attitudes will be shaken up and challenged.

When advising a course of action, this card suggests that you are in the mood for a risk, so take a gamble and try something new. Great faith and childlike trust in life are present now. The energies may be somewhat erratic and unstable, but their function is to dismantle what is outworn or outmoded. The tender shoots of new life need room to breathe; this is a period to clear the ground and see what comes up.

When signifying an individual, the Fool represents youth, unconventional approaches, spontaneous behaviour. As the first card in the cycle of the tarot trumps, it does not necessarily denote a young person – simply a youthful, unfettered spirit. Romantically, the Fool is usually someone who passes through your life, taking you by the hand and leading you towards an unknown future. Sexually unconventional people are often represented by this card – which symbolizes an androgynous being. Bisexuals, homosexuals, people in open marriages or other unusual arrangements may be signified. These meanings only apply when the card comes in answer to a relationship question, in a position which denotes the love life, or when accompanied by relationship cards, such as those from the suit of Cups.

Whether upright or reversed, the Fool can sometimes indicate tension, mental stress and fluctuating energy reserves. In the short term, this can be productive. As a way of life, it cannot be sustained.

Reversed Meaning

The Fool becomes unstable and unreliable when reversed. No practical risks should be taken, no binding financial arrangements nor speculative ventures embarked upon. Fortune may favour the brave but she is famously fickle, too. At this point, you would be foolish to risk anything you value.

When signifying a person, the reversed Fool is a tricky creature who cannot – with the best will in the world – offer you any kind of commitment or stability in business or love. He or she requires more freedom than you may be prepared to give, so think carefully before offering your heart or your money. If this person is already in your life, know that you cannot change them. Accept them for what they are, or bid them a fond farewell.

THE MAJOR ARCANA

I
THE MAGICIAN

RULING PLANET
Mercury

KEYWORDS
UPRIGHT: Initiation • Communication
REVERSED: Hesitation • Temporary blocks

CADUCEUS
is a symbol of all messenger gods and represents male and female energies

WINGED ARM
shows the Magician's ability to ascend to worlds above in shamanistic fashion

INFINITY SYMBOL
represents mathematical infinity and signifies the union between man and woman

WINGED FOOT
shows the Magician's ability to descend to worlds below

PLINTH
symbolizes the earth and material reality

MINOR ARCANA
symbols represent the four elements that were once believed to be the foundation of all life on earth

THE MAGICIAN

Symbolism of the Card

THE UNION OF OPPOSITES – ACTIVE AND RECEPTIVE, MALE AND FEMALE, INTELLECT AND INSTINCT – IS A CORE MEANING OF THE MAGICIAN, WHO CONTAINS ALL OPPOSITES WITHIN HIMSELF BECAUSE HE IS AN ANDROGYNOUS BEING.

The Magician raises one *winged arm* up towards the heavens, while the other points towards the earth, weighted down by a heavy pouch. One *foot* is winged also, and poised on tiptoe, as if to fly away. This symbolizes both the dual nature of the Magician and his ability to ascend to worlds above and descend to worlds below in truly shamanistic fashion. Winged wrists and ankles denote spirit, and are associated with the Greek messenger god, Hermes, or his Roman counterpart, Mercury. In alchemy, wings symbolize quicksilver, otherwise known as mercury, which is a volatile metal.

The Magician is associated with the planet *Mercury*; the sign or glyph for this planet is shown at the top of the two *caducei* or wands on each side of the figure. The caduceus with its two entwined serpents is a symbol of all messenger gods, of healing, and of male and female. For the alchemists, this symbol meant the blending of male fire and female water – the *solve et coagula* of alchemy, meaning 'dissolving and blending', which precedes transformation.

The Magician stands upon a *plinth*, symbolic of the earth and material reality. It is decorated with the symbols of the four suits of the *Minor Arcana* – the cup, wand, sword and pentacle – each in turn representing the four elements that were once believed to be the foundation of all life on earth. Above the Magician's head is the *infinity symbol*, a figure-of-eight lying on its side. This symbol represents mathematical infinity, and designates the equal forces of male and female energy – both are needed to make a whole. It is a symbol of union between man and woman – whether as lovers, or as the inner marriage of male and female within an individual's spirit.

The Shaman's Quest

Magic, especially the creation of amulets and talismans, beguiled and intrigued the educated minds of Renaissance Europe. Eagerly, they studied a range of intricate and mysterious knowledge – astrology, alchemy and ancient philosophies. The concept behind all magic, then and now, is age-old. It suggests that the world, tangible and invisible, can be influenced by ritual, spells, enchantments and by human power. A magician can mediate between the worlds, for he has travelled through them and returned with secret knowledge. He may command spirits to do his bidding, influence the weather, divine the future or, as an alchemist, turn base metal into gold. The Magician of the tarot begins to organize the wild energies signified by the Fool. He imposes order on chaos and juggles with elemental forces. In some decks this card is known as the Juggler, for the Magician has strong links with all tricksters, masters of illusion and showmen.

His symbolic ancestors are numerous, but at heart the Magician is a shaman, as are all shape-shifting spell-casters and healers. Shamans are visionaries, they visit unseen realms where they talk with spirits. The shaman knows how to loosen the bonds of reality, time, space and identity in order to create change and invite inspiration.

The alchemists, in turn, searched for ways to do just this; and there are many correspondences between the alchemical process and shamanistic ritual and exploration. The essence of alchemy is transformation. This can only be achieved by a number of processes, which always include the process of putrefaction and decay known as the nigredo, or blackening. This has been compared with depression, with apparent mental breakdown and with the experience of falling apart which must happen before true healing can begin. Following the nigredo are stages such as the rubedo, or reddening, where life triumphs and the alchemist knows that he or she is near to creating the elixir of life, or transforming base metal into gold. The mythic allure of alchemy as a philosophical quest must surely be based upon the journey of the archetypal shaman. Just as the shaman returns with secret knowledge, so the alchemist emerged from the laboratory, purified, cleansed and completely transformed by the ritual process.

There is a shamanistic figure at the living centre of every ancient way of life, a wise man or woman who has risked physical life and spiritual sanity to travel alone into the underworld, to encounter demons and even death itself in order to learn the secrets of life. The mystical revelations they experience are brought back to the daylight world, to enhance the lives of their community. The classic shamanistic pattern of descent, sacrifice, spiritual challenge and rebirth is part of mystery religions, mythic tales and the most powerful fairytales from all over the world. It is at least 30,000 years old, and its pattern and presence is the half-hidden blueprint for every true adventure. The path of the Fool through the complex stages of the tarot trumps is essentially shamanistic. The Magician represents his first guide.

THE MAGICIAN

Upright Meaning

The Magician signifies control over the visible world. This essential meaning may manifest in creative action, organizational skills, improved communications or an increased ability to focus on goals. Alluring dreams and playful fantasies are now brought out and examined. 'What can I do to make this happen?' 'What are my first steps towards this goal?' The Magician asks you to be realistic, yet full of optimistic hope and faith in the future. He does not pour cold water on your dreams, but suggests practical actions you might take towards them. A journey of a thousand miles begins with just one step, as the saying goes. The Magician often represents that step. And, as a symbol of language, talking, writing and negotiations, this card emphasizes the need to discuss your plans – if only with yourself.

When representing a person, the Magician signifies entrepreneurs, agents, psychotherapists, writers, linguists and anyone who speaks in public. If none of these categories seems appropriate, he denotes someone who will work a little practical magic for you – by introducing you to helpful people, by encouraging your talents, by giving you a book that inspires you, or by expanding your life in some lively and entertaining way. As a potential partner, the Magician is a witty individual with high levels of nervous energy. Often androgynous or bisexual, this character is more interested in conversation than in soulful, romantic interludes. Self-love is also symbolized – meaning that until you feel happy inside your own skin you will only attract partners who mirror your inadequacies, rather than someone who will enlarge your life and refresh your spirit.

Reversed Meaning

Plans and projects have ground to a halt when the Magician is reversed in a spread. This may be because you have over-analysed a creative impulse and taken the lifeblood out of it; because someone else is blocking your progress; or because you find yourself unable to make an important decision. Whatever the cause may be, it does not seem possible to complete a deal, project, business negotiation or to finalize travel plans at this point. Sometimes plans are blocked for a good reason – they may not be right for you. At other times, your own fears are causing the block and must be released for progress to continue. The surrounding cards will reveal more information.

THE MAJOR ARCANA

II
THE HIGH PRIESTESS

RULING PLANET
Moon

KEYWORDS
UPRIGHT: Intuition • Feminine mysteries
REVERSED: Secrets • Hidden factors

TREFOILS
symbolize material prosperity and point out towards the tangible outer world

CRESCENT MOON
represents the 'virgin' or autonomous state of the High Priestess

CAT
is a lunar creature and an ancient symbol of the feminine principle

CLOSED BOOK
suggests the wealth of knowledge she protects

POMEGRANATE
symbolizes the life-giving powers of the underworld

DOVES
are symbolic of the soul, peace and love

SERPENT
symbolizes wisdom, eternal life and secret knowledge

CROWN
is the crown of Isis, associating her with the archetypal goddess of ten thousand names

TWO PILLARS
guard the unconscious mind and mark the threshold to the underworld

Symbolism of the Card

AS A GUARDIAN OF THE THRESHOLD, THE HIGH PRIESTESS BELONGS IN TWO WORLDS – THE TANGIBLE, OUTER WORLD AND THE MYSTERIOUS, MOONLIT LAND OF DREAMS.

She is shown seated on a *crescent moon*, between *two pillars* that guard the hidden or unconscious mind. The silver sliver of the new moon represents her 'virgin' or autonomous state, for she is self-contained and, like the moon, she regenerates herself.

At the foot of one column we see a *cat*, a lunar creature, anciently symbolic of the feminine principle. A gleaming green serpent winds up the other column. The *serpent* symbolizes wisdom, eternal life and secret knowledge. It was a companion of the prophetic sibyls of ancient Greece, and has always been associated with goddesses in Europe and the Middle East.

Atop each column is a *dove*, symbolic of the soul, of peace and of love. One old gypsy legend says that the souls of their female ancestors are transformed into doves, while the men become serpents. The High Priestess rules the underworld, or unconscious, and so is also associated with the idea of the invisible soul or spirit of a person – their secret potential or essence.

In the High Priestess's hand rests a juicy red *pomegranate*. This exotic fruit combines both sweet and bitter tastes, and was the only fruit said to grow in the underworld, where it was eaten by the souls of the dead in order to be reborn. The pomegranate is associated with Persephone, the Greek goddess of the underworld, who swallowed some seeds and so had to remain for part of each year in the land of the dead as a bride of Hades. The High Priestess carries this fruit to symbolize the life-giving powers of the underworld. Through dreams and intuition, she offers us inspiration and the ability to transcend our everyday problems and concerns.

The *closed book* that rests on her lap suggests the wealth of knowledge she protects; knowledge that is available only to those who are prepared to risk the journey into her shadowy realms and to taste her special, bittersweet fruit.

The Mistress of Mystery

The High Priestess is the guardian of secrets, seated at the threshold to the underworld. She is linked with the slender curve of the crescent moon, which rules the virgin or veiled aspect of the goddess. In this guise, she is the mistress of mystery who challenges anyone who approaches her. She is the first gateway on the Major Arcana's eternal journey of self-knowledge.

With the passing of centuries, and the rise of religions dominated by a male deity, perceptions of the goddess became fragmented. Her alluring essence could be glimpsed, however, in a rich array of legends, fables and obscure philosophies, such as alchemy. The High Priestess can be linked with the Queen of Sheba, who brought all the wealth of the East to King Solomon; with winged Lilith, goddess of the night, who was biblical Adam's fabled first wife; and with Sara-Kali, patron saint of the gypsies, who is said to have accompanied Mary Magdalene on a perilous sea voyage to France. These figures are all incorporated in her image.

The core meaning of tarot's High Priestess is secret wisdom. She is also an independent and powerful being – autonomous in the way of the earliest-known goddess figures. Her origins lie with the great goddess of 10,000 names, whose true identity is Egyptian Black Isis in her veiled form. Isis was venerated in Paris and Rome for many centuries. Aspects of her were eventually concealed and fragmented in a number of other figures, such as the enigmatic Black Madonnas who have puzzled scholars all over Europe. Old legends of Sara-Kali, or Saint Sarah, for example, assert that Mary Magdalene and her 'Egyptian maid', Sara, were notably independent women with secret knowledge.

Bird-footed Lilith, too, was a powerful symbol of rebellion and autonomy. In her demonic guise, she ate unprotected children and seduced men away from their wives. She brought storm and chaos in her wake. In the thirteenth century she was said to offer the gift of prophecy to those who respected her. The High Priestess is also an intuitive woman, and often indicates the stirrings of intuition when she appears in a spread.

The fabulously wealthy Queen of Sheba also possessed great wisdom and power which she was willing to share with King Solomon, who cured her of her bird's foot disfigurement with his magic powers – she is believed to be a development of the myth of Lilith. Similarly, the High Priestess brings great riches with her – treasures that are held within the unconscious mind.

Upright Meaning

Like the moon, which shines at night but is sometimes just visible in the sky during the day, the High Priestess may manifest in the inner or outer world, or both. Fundamentally, she signifies secrets, hidden knowledge and the forces of intuition. She advises you to listen to your own inner voice, to the promptings of instinct and intuition. If you are seeking guidance, you will find it through focusing on your dreams and your waking intuitive feelings. This is not a time to rely on logic alone, but it is a positive time to consult oracles or keep a dream diary.

In the tangible world, the High Priestess denotes powerful women who may be able to offer you help or inspiration. She may represent your mother, your boss, a healer, a psychic or a therapist. In a man's cards she represents the unobtainable, a woman he idealizes who can never be more than a seductive fantasy. She can also symbolize the inner feminine principle, which for both men and women is the creative spring that enriches our lives.

When you draw this card, you must also draw breath and be prepared to wait a while. This is no time to force a decision, or to rely on factual information. Nothing is quite what it seems at the moment. Hidden forces are casting a subtle influence over your affairs, so try to bide your time until the full picture emerges into the bright light indicated by the next card in the Major Arcana, the Empress.

Reversed Meaning

The High Priestess reversed denotes distortion, deception, illusion and spiritual blindness. When inner promptings are being ignored or suppressed, they may wreak havoc or lead to depression and lack of vitality.

Reversed, the High Priestess warns you that you may be losing touch with reality. This can manifest in superficial relationships, false friends and clandestine activities. Hidden enemies are traditionally signified by this card – you may have suppressed doubts regarding these individuals. In business or personal relationships you must ask yourself: 'What were my initial impressions?' 'What do I really feel?' Since the High Priestess rules secret knowledge, you must step into her world to find the answers. As with the upright position, do not enter into any binding agreements now or make any decisions you cannot alter in the future.

THE MAJOR ARCANA

III
THE EMPRESS

RULING PLANET
Venus

KEYWORDS
UPRIGHT: Creativity • Fertility • Harvest
REVERSED: Lack • Repressed energy

VINES
can symbolize the fertility of the Tree of Life

GRAPES
have links with Dionysus, god of the vine, and with Demeter's Eleusinian Mysteries

VENUS
is associated in astrology with love, relationships, artistic taste and beauty

HORNS OF PLENTY
are powerful symbols of fruitfulness, endless supply and bountiful creativity

SHEAF OF WHEAT
is an ancient symbol of abundance and fertility

Symbolism of the Card

THE EMPRESS, LIKE ALL DIVINE MYTHIC QUEENS, IS CROWNED WITH STARS. THIS IS A PARTICULAR ATTRIBUTE OF VENUS/APHRODITE, GODDESS OF LOVE AND RELATIONSHIPS, WHO HAS DEEP CONNECTIONS WITH THIS CARD.

She is shown rising from a *sheaf of wheat* or corn, an ancient symbol of abundance and fertility. In ancient Greece a sheaf of grain was the central symbol of the Mysteries at Eleusis, where the great earth mother, Demeter, was celebrated. All over the world, grain and bread have symbolized life, provision for the future and the fruits of agricultural labours. Venus/Aphrodite was, originally, a goddess of plants and cultivated places. Here, she represents the creative fertility and sense of renewal which are the essence of this beautiful image.

Grain and *vines* with bunches of ripe *grapes* are anciently linked in many cultures. The vine is sometimes symbolic of the Tree of Life, and its fertility associated with passion and abundance – these are all important attributes of the Empress. Grapes, and the wine we make from them, are linked to Dionysus, god of the vine, and also to Demeter's Mysteries – where the infant Dionysus appeared. Bread and wine together mean hospitality, generosity and sharing life's good things with loved ones.

Here the vines spring up from two *horns of plenty* or cornucopias – a symbol of both male and female, being both phallic and receptive. Cornucopias are powerful symbols of fruitfulness, endless supply and bountiful creativity. They were associated with Demeter, and also with Fortuna, where they poured out the blessings of a benign fate upon the fortunate. This feeling of expansion and receiving life's most vibrant gifts is central to the Empress in interpretation. The Empress cradles the astrological glyph for the planet Venus in her hand. *Venus* rules this card; in astrology it is associated with love and relationships, artistic taste and personal style, beauty and adornment, money, balance and partnerships.

The Fertile Bride

The Empress is placed beside her virginal maiden sister, the High Priestess. In some decks she is called Juno, after the Roman wife of the god Jupiter, patroness of marriage and families, whose sacred month was June – a traditional time for weddings. In decks created around the time of the French Revolution she is called the Grandmother – an ancient goddess title. The card of the Empress is usually interpreted to mean fertility, pregnancy and sometimes marriage. The Empress is numbered three. This number is traditionally associated with goddesses because it represents creativity springing from the duality signified by two. It is also symbolic of the three kingdoms which belonged to the goddesses of old – queen of heaven, of the earth and its creatures, and of the shadowy underworld. The archetypal goddess generally has three main aspects: maiden, bride/mother and crone. These deities were given different names, but are all aspects of the same powerful figure who could create and destroy life on earth.

In Greek mythology, to give one example, Demeter is the mother goddess who has dominion over the earth's fertility. Her daughter, Kore, represents her maiden aspect, while Persephone is her dark, death goddess name. Demeter's temple at Eleusis was the scene of a flourishing pagan mystery religion for 2000 years. Officially eradicated in the fourth or fifth century AD, there is evidence that Greek peasants were still offering tributes to Demeter during the nineteenth century.

The Eleusinian Mysteries offered devotees initiation and the promise of resurrection after death. The ceremonies were carried out in darkness, then the initiate was led, blinking, into the daylight. This mirrored the cycle of the European seasons, when winter creates a dark, lifeless landscape and summer seems a distant dream. Then spring arrives, with all its miraculous fecundity, and clothes the earth. It is hardly surprising that such a force was believed to be magical, mysterious and feminine. Indeed, the earliest fertility goddesses were parthenogenic; that is, they conceived their offspring unaided. Later, goddesses acquired consorts whose lifespan was often short and sweet – they were sacrificed, just as crops are harvested, on an annual basis.

By the Renaissance, Christianity had suppressed much of the old ritual and religion. However, it merely transformed itself, flowing underground and reappearing in Gnostic heresies, alchemy, magic, mystical philosophies, fairytales and legends. Glorious images of the once-great goddess appeared in art – Botticelli's *The Birth of Venus* and *Primavera* remain world-famous Renaissance paintings celebrating feminine deities. And within the orthodox Church the Virgin Mary assimilated many of the titles – such as Queen of Heaven – once accorded to Egyptian Isis, Sumerian Ishtar and a host of others. Crowned with stars, like Venus/Aphrodite, the Virgin Mary represented the longed-for feminine principle, albeit in sanitized form. The tarot's Empress expresses the power and sensuality of the ancient goddesses, a message that is underlined by her pairing with the Star, a symbol of the goddess revealed.

THE EMPRESS

Upright Meaning

Fertility and abundance are the keynotes of this sensual card. It evokes the warmth of summer and the scent of fruits and flowers, because the Empress is the embodiment of life itself. When such a vibrant image materializes in a reading it is especially important to examine the context in which it appears, for in the real world the Empress represents the many faces of creativity and fertility.

The simplest interpretation of the Empress is marriage and motherhood. As pagan bride and earth mother, the Empress signifies loving union and pregnancy. Naturally, these traditional meanings cannot apply to everyone, nor to every reading in which this card appears. Fertility of the mind and spirit are, therefore, important meanings to consider, too. 'Brainchild' is a term we often use when describing an inspiration or compelling idea. A creative project, such as a painting, book, craftwork or poem, is a brainchild – as is a business venture, an invention or a sudden desire to bake a home-made loaf of bread. The impulse to create something life-enhancing is signified by this card, and such inner vitality may express itself in numerous ways.

When representing a person, the Empress is a sensual, passionate woman. She may be a lover, muse or inspirational and beloved friend. She is the outer image of your own creativity, sensuality and abundant vitality. When denoting a love affair, the Empress represents an intense, tender and tactile relationship – a grand passion, a great love.

Reversed Meaning

As the great mother goddesses of mythology were said to create winter when they descended to the underworld each year, so the reversed Empress signifies a period of lack, sterility and spiritual stagnation in someone's life. This position suggests physical infertility, impotence and other sexual difficulties within a relationship. Where other cards affirm, the Empress reversed can denote destructive promiscuity, unwanted babies and abusive sexual relationships where power ploys have replaced love and feelings of spontaneity.

On other levels, when this card is reversed it suggests creative blocks, loss of energy and a lack of interest in the present moment. Discomfort in the material world, through actual poverty or through simple problems such as a leaking roof or troublesome neighbours, can also be denoted. Companion cards will clarify the context, and some small but luxurious pleasure may help to begin the healing process.

IV
THE EMPEROR

RULING SIGN
Aries

KEYWORDS
UPRIGHT: Structure • Success • Ambition
REVERSED: Loss of control

EAGLES are emblems of numerous sky gods and symbolize power, royalty and strength

ORB AND SCEPTRE symbolize the Emperor's status as consort to the Empress

HORN SYMBOLS echo the Emperor's associations with the planet Mars, the sign of Aries and the phallic powers they represent

HORNED CROWN underlines the Emperor's masculinity and suggests the virility of all the warrior gods

DEEP RED clothes represent the Emperor's mature energy

SNAILS symbolize the feminine, lunar energies upon which the Emperor's edifice rests

LEGS in the figure-four position echo the solid number of this card

Symbolism of the Card

THE EMPEROR BRINGS A NOTE OF SOMBRE MASCULINITY TO THE PROCESSION OF THE TAROT TRUMPS. AS THE FIRST ESSENTIALLY MALE FIGURE, HE SIGNIFIES ACTIVE, OUTGOING AND CONSTRUCTIVE ENERGIES.

The Emperor stands with his *legs* in the figure-four position, traditional to this card. It represents the astrological glyph for the planet Jupiter, another name for the Emperor, and also echoes the solid number of his card.

The Emperor holds an *orb and sceptre*, symbols of male and female, and symbols of his rank and status as consort to the Empress. In this design, horn symbols spring from both objects, echoing this card's associations with the planet Mars, the sign of Aries, and the phallic powers they both represent. The Emperor's *crown* also bears decorative horns, underlining the essential masculinity of his presence and suggesting the virility of all warrior gods. They also link him with the Empress, for horns are both solar and lunar symbols, and are connected with mother goddesses in myriad mythologies.

Clothed in the *deep red* of mature energy, the Emperor surveys his kingdom, framed by two columns of diamond shapes. *Horn symbols* decorate the base of these columns, beneath them *snails* symbolize the feminine, lunar energies upon which the whole edifice rests. Without an awareness of the soul, which is the feminine principle symbolized by the Empress, the Emperor's powers will crumble to dust. Atop each pillar an *eagle* stretches out one wing to form a canopy over the figure of the Emperor. The eagle is an emblem of numerous sky gods, a dizzying array of them in fact, including Hindu Vishnu, Scandinavian Odin, Greek Zeus and Roman Jupiter. This bird is a symbol of power, royalty, strength, good fortune and inspiration. As such, it was a favourite symbol of the Roman emperors, and appears in many tarot designs for this card.

Earthly Powers

The Emperor, consort of the Empress, represents masculine power, creative potency and the forces of the material world. His number is four, the number of foundation, stability, structure and tangible form. As the Fool continues his journey, he encounters the world of matter, structure and action that the Emperor represents.

Some decks name him Jupiter, husband to Juno. Many old tarot designs show his legs in the figure-four position, which resembles the astrological glyph for the planet Jupiter. In the Charles VI tarot deck he is shown with a sceptre bearing the fleur-de-lis, a symbol of French royalty that is also a symbol of the goddess Juno, whose magical lily fertilized her and created the god Mars. As the Grandfather in the French Revolutionary deck, he clutches a three-petalled flower, reminiscent of a fleur-de-lis.

This card is linked with Mars in later decks, making the Emperor a mythic and astrological partner of Venus, the Empress. The god Mars was originally associated with fertility and, as king consort, was sacrificed each March to ensure growth and fertility for the rest of the year. As one of Venus' mythical lovers, he fathered Harmony, the peace-bringer. Harmonious creation requires both active and receptive energies, which are signified by the Emperor and Empress respectively.

The aggressive, destructive aspects of the Emperor are found in mythic tales of war-like Mars, and Jupiter's fondness for hurling thunderbolts around. When signifying reason without intuition or feeling, the Emperor may be cold and cruel, preferring domination over co-operation, and war over peace. Some scholars assert that the pairing of the Emperor with the Tower is a clear fourteenth-century political message prophesying the decline and fall of the Holy Roman Empire. Others suggest a Gnostic theme – all worldly power and riches are only temporary, death and destruction await those who lose sight of this.

The notion of karmic retribution, of pride coming before a fall, is very old and may be found in numerous mythologies peopled with jealous deities and vengeful Fates. The Emperor's power is only temporary, his true kingdom may only be reached through the Empress – just as ancient Irish kings, and Sumerians before them, symbolically married the goddess before they were considered fit to rule.

This theme of power without fertility is found in the Rider Waite deck. Here the Emperor is shown in a barren kingdom of rocky mountains – a place where the fertility of the Empress cannot penetrate. Since, as consort, his ancient fate was death by sacrifice, this may also represent the futility of a kingdom ruled by a lone male god. Without the Empress, his creative gifts cannot flower or bear fruit. The king and queen of alchemy – Sol and Luna – were always represented as indivisible; the solar and lunar powers were both needed to bring the alchemical work to its conclusion. The Emperor and his Empress are the king and queen of the tarot, and their magical wedding is represented by the Lovers. As a fiery male figure, the Emperor seeks the cool waters and timeless wisdom of the Empress. As the tarot trumps unfold, the Fool comes to realize that both qualities are needed for maturity and development.

THE EMPEROR

Upright Meaning

The Emperor is very much a card of the material world, representing power, ambition and the drive for visible success in life. He may simply signify that this is a time in your life when you must assert yourself, make practical plans and deal with authority figures in a responsible manner. The Emperor can represent authority in a number of ways – manifesting as government departments, multinational companies, the armed forces or other large and powerful organizations. People associated with these organizations may also be symbolized by the Emperor. On a more personal level, any male figure with power or authority may appear as the Emperor. He may be your boss, your father or even your landlord. When denoting yourself, or your enquirer, he suggests an increase of some kind – a promotion at work, power over others' welfare, control over a project or event, or simply an increase in ambition and drive.

As a figure in your life, the Emperor often represents someone with wealth and substance. Successful men, especially those in control of companies or organizations, tend to be signified. Other cards will tell you how and why this person is affecting you. As a relationship card, the Emperor represents a man whose silent strength masks repressed emotions. He has passion and charisma, but will dominate his friends and loved ones at every opportunity. It may be impossible to know what he is feeling, although individuals of this type will rarely stay in an unsatisfying partnership for long – their need for success in all areas is so strong that they cannot compromise in matters of the heart.

Reversed Meaning

Issues of power and control are emphasized when the Emperor is reversed. Some kind of power struggle may take place at work, or in your relationship or a close friendship. You may find yourself picking your way through a maze of rules and regulations, or dealing with the law in some way. Adopt a positive attitude towards this if you can, and try not to battle against authority at this time – whether this means your boss, your father or the taxman.

When the reversed Emperor refers to you, you may find yourself losing your own authority and drive. Loss of power may manifest in low energy, loss of interest in your work or an inability to assert yourself. As a card describing an individual, it warns you against a cold, calculating man who is using you for his own reasons.

THE MAJOR ARCANA

— V —
THE HIEROPHANT

RULING SIGN
Taurus

KEYWORDS
UPRIGHT: Gateway to knowledge
REVERSED: Rebellion • Anarchy

STONE ACORNS symbolize potential because they contain the pattern of the oak tree

TWIN PILLARS echo the Hierophant's meaning of a bridge or gateway

VINE LEAVES link the Hierophant with the card of the Devil

EYE is protective and represents wisdom, all-seeing knowledge and the doorway to spiritual knowledge

BULL'S HORNS link the Hierophant with the astrological sign of Taurus and also with the High Priestess

KNEELING FIGURES represent the Hierophant's acolytes and the need to blend the opposing energies of action and receptivity

Symbolism of the Card

THE HIEROPHANT, OR POPE, SYMBOLIZES THE RULER OF THE SPIRITUAL WORLD, JUST AS THE EMPEROR PRESIDES OVER THE MATERIAL WORLD.

The Hierophant represents a bridge or gateway, as suggested by the *twin pillars* that mark the doors into his world. These are decorated with twining *vine leaves* to reveal his links with the card of the Devil, a figure made of leaves. The Hierophant represents logical, conventional thinking, while his mystical counterpart symbolizes the forces of chaos and anarchy. Atop each pillar is a large *stone acorn*, symbolic of potential, because it holds within it the pattern of the mighty oak tree into which it will grow. The Fool must pass through this gateway on his journey, and the acorns suggest the seeds of the great adventure that lies ahead.

Beneath the Hierophant's feet is a plinth. Two *kneeling figures* are carved upon it, representing the Hierophant's acolytes and also the opposing energies of action and receptivity that must blend harmoniously together to create a whole. This recurrent tarot theme is fully pictured in the card of the Lovers, which follows this one. Here, in the Hierophant, the mystical marriage is simply hinted at.

The Hierophant wears a headdress with *bull's horns*, suggesting this card's links with the astrological sign of Taurus, the Bull. The curving horns also link this figure with the High Priestess, because they echo the shape of a crescent moon, her most important symbol. Bulls symbolize many things, but bull-headed male figures generally guard gateways, treasures or sacred places in myth – just as the Hierophant is seated at the gateway to his spiritual kingdom. Above him, the *eye* within the triangle represents wisdom, all-seeing knowledge and the doorway to spiritual knowledge. It is protective and purposeful, just as this card sometimes symbolizes the acquisition of knowledge for a purpose.

The Divine Bull

The Hierophant, or Pope, bears the number five, which signifies matter infused by spirit. He is the alchemical Philosopher's Stone, capable of revealing the pure gold of inspiration and wisdom. The title 'Hierophant' was the name given to the high priest at the Eleusinian Mysteries in ancient Greece, where Demeter was celebrated as the great goddess of fertility, and where Dionysus, god of wine and ecstasy, appeared as an infant saviour, tucked up in a winnowing basket.

These links between the ostensibly Christian world of Renaissance Europe and the ancient anarchy signified by Dionysus are hinted at by the pairing of the Hierophant with the Devil, who is, himself, an image of the old horned god of pagan times. Indeed, in one eighteenth-century deck, this card is named Bacchus, the Roman counterpart of Dionysus. Dionysus was a saviour god who promised resurrection to his followers. Torn to pieces, dismembered in various ways in various myths, Dionysus was restored to life by his grandmother, Rhea, archetypal earth mother. His creatures include leopards, stags and bulls. This card is said to be ruled by Taurus, the sign of the Bull.

It is the bull that neatly connects the symbolic Pope with a larger-than-life Renaissance figure. Pope Alexander VI was a prominent member of the notoriously dangerous, amoral Borgia clan, whose legends are awash with illegitimate children and mysterious murders, and who were said to possess expert knowledge of poisons. During the 1490s, Alexander commissioned the artist Pinturicchio to paint a series of Egyptian scenes in the Vatican.

These included the Apis Bull, the symbol of the dismembered and resurrected Osiris, also an heraldic symbol of the turbulent Borgias themselves. Osiris was the brother, son and lover of Isis, whose mysteries and teachings are linked with the card of the High Priestess – just as the Hierophant is connected with the High Priestess in the tarot. These two figures wield power in the spiritual realms, while the Emperor and Empress embody the pleasures of reality.

At first glance, the Hierophant simply represents the head of the Christian Church, a powerful force in Renaissance times. A little investigation soon reveals hints that this is merely skimming the surface of a seething cauldron whose contents are ancient, disturbing and anarchic. Renaissance popes were, on the whole, colourful figures – rarely celibate, often interested in the study of magic and astrology, sensual and worldly. While this card is frequently interpreted to signify conventional belief, organized religion and sometimes established organizations in general, its links with wilder ideas and with pagan practices are undeniable.

Upright Meaning

This card represents a formal gateway in your life. Whether this leads to marriage or education – this card's traditional meanings – will be clarified by the surrounding images in the reading. When it symbolizes education, the Hierophant denotes both teachers and students. It invariably represents formal knowledge, universities,

THE HIEROPHANT

established colleges and all courses that lead to recognized qualifications. The emphasis tends towards intellectual studies rather than practical achievements, although a significant group of Pentacles in the spread could change this interpretation. The Hierophant also symbolizes religious groups, orthodox religious beliefs and the personal need for ritual and ceremony. The position of the card will reveal whether this applies to you or to someone in your life.

When signifying marriage, the Hierophant represents the public ceremony and acknowledgement of love and commitment rather than the private, emotional bonds that exist between two people. The union of families, the sharing and shaping of destinies, and the drama of the marriage rites are embodied within this card. Sometimes Justice or the Ace of Pentacles appears with the Hierophant when this meaning is appropriate to your reading.

As an individual, the Hierophant often stands for an older friend, teacher or spiritual adviser. Their advice is balanced and helpful. This is someone who can open up your mind and educate your heart.

As a card of character and personality, the Hierophant tends towards the conventional. He represents a profound need for routine, certainty, security and tradition. Spontaneous gestures may alarm this person, while lack of financial security is probably their worst nightmare. If this card refers to you, you may need to create a regular routine for yourself – or simply put your possessions and personal belongings in order.

Reversed Meaning

The Hierophant reversed turns conventional ideas and behaviour upside down. Some kind of rebellion is signified. This may manifest as eccentricity or as a powerful urge to be an iconoclast – to break all the rules and lead a very different kind of life from the one you have known until now. Rejecting parental values, and especially your parents' chosen religion, is a common meaning of this card – you may feel that your background has little or nothing to offer you in adult life, so you decide to live by your own rules and to create your own morality.

The reversed Hierophant also represents unsound advice, usually from an official, lawyer, accountant or spiritual adviser. Do not be impressed by their position or title, and do not be rushed into making any kind of formal agreement at this time. These warnings also apply to any investments, savings schemes or expensive purchases that you may be considering at the time of the reading. Wait a while before committing yourself.

VI
THE LOVERS

RULING SIGN
Gemini

KEYWORDS
UPRIGHT: Love • Choice
REVERSED: Disrupted emotions

SOL
symbolizes the fiery forces of heat, light and the principle of masculine action known as yang

WHITE ROSES
represent light, purity, beauty and mystery

RED ROSES
signify a passionate heart and embody the idea of romance and seduction

WINGED CHERUB
is the spirit of Cupid or Eros and symbolizes the unpredictability and ancient anarchy of love

LUNA
typifies receptive, cold, moist lunar energies and the principle of feminine action known as yin

Symbolism of the Card

THE RENAISSANCE TAROT'S UNDERLYING ALCHEMICAL THEME IS, PERHAPS, MOST CLEARLY REVEALED BY THE LOVERS – A CARD THAT PRESENTS THE UNIVERSAL ARCHETYPE OF LOVE, BALANCE AND THE UNION OF OPPOSITES.

The eponymous lovers of this card are shown here as *Sol* and *Luna* – the alchemical king and queen who represent the sun and moon. Sol, with his symbolic sun face, symbolizes the fiery forces of heat, light and the masculine action principle. Chinese philosophy and medicine names this energy as yang. Luna, the queen whose head is formed by a symbolic moon, typifies receptive, cold, moist lunar energies – called yin by the Chinese. In alchemy, Sol and Luna need each other to create a whole, just as an entire earth day begins with the rising sun and ends with the moon lighting the night sky. So Sol wears a necklace bearing a crescent moon, while Luna's ornament is a miniature sun – symbolizing their indivisible equality with one another.

A traditional *winged cherub*, the spirit of Cupid or Eros, is placed above the alchemical couple. Eros became known as Aphrodite's son in later mythology but originally he was born of the forces of Night and Chaos. On this card he symbolizes the unpredictability and ancient anarchy of love. He draws back his arrow, preparing to shoot love's darts into their hearts. Once these darts have found their mark, nothing can be done to change their effect.

Red and *white roses* twine together up each side of the image – red for the masculine sun and white for the feminine moon. In alchemy, roses signify wisdom and wholeness. Red and white roses together symbolize the marriage of fire and water, further amplifying the core message of this card. Red roses signify a passionate heart, embodying the idea of romance and seduction, while white roses stand for light, purity, beauty and mystery. A number of traditions say that roses spring from the Tree of Life itself, which flourished in the heart of the gardens of Paradise.

The Magical Wedding

The unambiguous title of this card reveals its core meaning. Yet there are deeper layers to be discovered, too, in the meaning of the Lovers. The number of this card is six, a number of Venus, meaning harmony with underlying tensions – this is reflected in this card's significance as a card of choice. As a card of loving union, it presents an erotic and pagan message – one which was certainly not approved of by the established Church at the time that these cards first appeared. Indeed, some early versions of the tarot, the Lovers card depicts a young couple being married by an older woman or priestess – this is a Gnostic theme, springing from traditional ancient rituals and ceremonies. In most cards, Cupid or an angel hovers over the scene, to represent the higher powers that are involved in true love's course. In addition, such figures signify the spiritual union of male and female that can take place within every individual's soul. Once blended, or married to one another, they then yield up a third energy – the united spirit, the authentic self.

The theme of mystical, magical weddings finds a fascinating example in alchemy. The marriage of the sun and the moon, as Sol and Luna respectively, is one of the key themes of the old alchemical texts where it is called the Chymical Wedding. This wedding of the watery, feminine forces of Luna with the fiery, male energies of Sol is variously a metaphor for a chemical reaction, a spiritual quest or a psychological process, and hints at an oriental sexual philosophy, such as Tantra. Tantric secrets, and the belief that a spiritual–sexual union led to enlightenment, inform much alchemical symbolism and are found in Courtly Love poetry of the fourteenth century.

Here is a small extract from a lengthy alchemical poem that was first published in the 1400s:

O Luna,
surrounded by me/
and sweet one mine/

You become
fine/strong/and
powerful as I am

O Sol/you are
recognizable
above all others/

You need me as
the cock needs the
hens.

The magical child that the royal couple conceive is an hermaphrodite, often shown above the couple – as winged Cupid is shown above them on the tarot card. Again, the hermaphrodite represents the ultimate blending of male and female energies to create a whole – both needing the other to unite the opposites that they embody. This card offers another alchemical allusion because it is paired with Temperance, a winged figure blending liquids between two vessels in truly alchemical fashion. The Fool's journey has brought him to outward maturity and the knowledge of a loving relationship. He must now choose between what he has learned so far, and the lure of further adventures and discoveries.

THE LOVERS

Upright Meaning

At first glance, the Lovers would seem to be a simple image to interpret. Indeed, at one level, it is. When supported by the suit of Cups, or perhaps the Empress, this card signifies love, attraction, romance and dazzling chemistry between two people. Any relationship it denotes is intimate and memorable – but it is certainly not a card of marriage. As a relationship card, the Lovers promises an intense involvement of mind, body and spirit. What happens thereafter is another matter entirely – ancient myths were very clear on this point. Erotic, romantic love was often very separate from the sensible arrangements that accompanied a formal marriage contract. So the Lovers represents the unruly, unpredictable arrows of desire.

Secondly, the Lovers is a card of choice. And just as the choice of a romantic partner may seem to be out of our control, so the choice represented here is an emotional and intuitive one. Typically, the choice represented is between following the path you have already decided upon, and taking some kind of risk or gamble with the unknown. There are no penalties for staying put, but you are being offered an opportunity to explore something new. Other cards will describe what this might be, but nothing except your own intuition can tell you which path to choose at this point. Assessing your life, dreams and hopes will help you to make the decision – and this is the whole point, for the choice presented to you is not a crossroads in life but a way of waking you up to life's myriad possibilities. In almost every situation there is a choice, although we may not always be aware of it. This is one of those times when it is crystal clear.

Reversed Meaning

Traditionally, the Lovers reversed signifies love triangles, clandestine affairs and infidelity. This meaning is confirmed by the Three of Swords, but it is usually made clear by the general tone and setting of the reading in which it appears. If you are embarking upon a new relationship it offers a warning – do you know if your intended partner is available? He or she may not be as free as you think. You may feel compelled to become involved with someone outside your usual relationship. There is often a magnetic pull between two people when this card appears, and it can be almost impossible to resist or deny. The end of a relationship may be signified, but rarely without an affair or memories of a past involvement triggering the breakup.

THE MAJOR ARCANA

VII
THE CHARIOT

RULING SIGN
Cancer

KEYWORDS
UPRIGHT: Victory after struggle
REVERSED: Waste • Limitations

CRESCENT MOONS
connect this card with its ruling sign of Cancer and symbolize new beginnings

CRAB
is a lunar symbol associated with death and dreams, thereby linking this card with the Death card

SILVER
represents the receptive energies present in every spirit, life story and symbolic system throughout the world

BLACK
represents the active energies present in every spirit, life story and symbolic system throughout the world

GRIFFINS
are fabled creatures that represent watchfulness, strength, power and fate

Symbolism of the Card

THE CHARIOT AND ITS DRIVER REPRESENT VICTORY AND HEROIC STATUS IN NUMEROUS MYTHOLOGIES. THE CHARIOTEER – OFTEN A DIVINE BEING – SYMBOLIZES THE MIND DIRECTING AND MASTERMINDING THE ACTIONS OF LIFE.

The mind's thoughts and mode of action are represented by the creatures that draw the chariot – so white horses, a solar symbol, draw the chariot of the sun god, Apollo, across the sky, while doves, symbols of affection, pull the chariot of Venus/Aphrodite.

Griffins draw the chariot on this tarot trump. A complex symbol, they have been chosen here to represent watchfulness, strength, power and fate. Griffins, like dragons, often guarded fabled treasures and thus were ever-vigilant. One creature is *black*, the other *silver*, representing the active and receptive energies present in every spirit, every life story and every symbolic system throughout the world. This innate duality has been encountered in the previous card, the Lovers; it is an important underlying theme in the tarot's symbolism.

Twin *crescent moons* decorate the shoulders of the charioteer, connecting this card with its ruling sign of Cancer, the Crab, whose natal planet is the moon. They are also symbols of new beginnings, as the moon renews itself each month throughout the year. The Chariot means victory, and also ushers in a new phase, asking 'What next?'

The *crab* underlines these connections with the zodiac sign of Cancer the Crab, the sign of the summer solstice that takes place at the end of June in the northern hemisphere. As a lunar symbol, it is associated with death and dreams, linking this card to its mystical partner, Death. In many of the world's mythologies, the lover of the great goddess traditionally died each year after the summer solstice, to be reborn or recovered from the underworld days or weeks later.

The Lord of Time

The Chariot is commonly drawn by two horses, and by two sphinxes in some later decks. For *The Renaissance Tarot* we have chosen a pair of griffins to draw the Lord of Time's vehicle. The fables and legends surrounding these exotic hybrids are especially relevant to the seventh tarot trump card – and also to the Renaissance period.

A fabulous beast of tremendous strength, the griffin originated in the Near East – Mesopotamia, Egypt and India. It became a great favourite in heraldry, where it means strength and vigilance. In ancient Greece griffins were sacred to Apollo, god of the sun, and his sister, the moon. They appeared with Athene, symbolizing wisdom, and with Nemesis, goddess of fate, as vengeance. Ancient Roman artists showed Nemesis riding in a chariot drawn by griffins – an implacable goddess accompanied by her fierce creatures.

The Italian Renaissance poet, Dante, wrote in *The Divine Comedy* that griffins represented 'the mystic shape that joins the two natures in one form'. The Chariot follows the Lovers, a card symbolizing the impulse to unite masculine and feminine energies to create a whole. The two creatures on this card are said to represent heart and mind, body and soul, reason and desire. When tamed or understood, these qualities join forces to refine and strengthen the spirit.

Griffins were undoubtedly very fearsome creatures, often associated with potentially hostile or destructive forces. The Chariot sometimes warns against the misuse of power and talent – two energies that can become destructive if they are not controlled. Griffins could, however, be tamed, and their powers were subsequently used to protect valuable treasures. Mesopotamian griffins were often shown with the Master or Mistress of the Griffins, who either stood between them or rode in a chariot behind them.

A popular medieval legend developed out of these pagan fables. Alexander the Great was said to have ridden high above the world in an airborne chariot drawn by griffins. The victorious Renaissance rulers of city–states adopted the triumphal chariot – copying the heroes of classical antiquity by entering the city in a triumphal car and driving prisoners of war before them. Charioteers generally symbolize victory, but also time, and the measure of the day and of life itself.

This card's number, seven, is a number of the moon, which completes a quarter of its monthly cycle every seven days. Moon calendars were one of the earliest ways that human beings recorded the passage of time. Appropriately, the esoteric ruler of the Chariot is the sign of Cancer. This moon-ruled sign begins at the summer solstice, when the sun rides triumphant in the summer sky, just as Apollo was pictured riding triumphantly across the heavens in his golden chariot. With the Chariot a cycle has been completed, much has been learned, but the descent to encounter the tarot's more challenging figures has yet to be made.

THE CHARIOT

Upright Meaning

Of all the early cards of the Major Arcana, the Chariot is perhaps the most complicated to interpret. We tend, today, to think of time as an entirely linear progression. In terms of tarot symbolism and other mystical teachings, this is a fallacy. Such philosophies picture time as an eternal spiral, endlessly circling above and below itself, defined by endings and beginnings throughout life's path. So it is with the Chariot, which at its simplest means victory after a lengthy struggle. However, although all the best fairytales end 'happily ever after', life is not like this. Sooner or later, the question 'Now what?' must be asked. This is why traditional interpretations of the Chariot stressed caution in victory, for energy and focus will be needed in the days ahead to forge a new path, and to develop in fresh, and perhaps surprising, ways.

The success and joy promised by the Chariot invariably come after a great deal of effort, hard work and soul-searching. There is no hint of an overnight success or a sudden turn of fortune here. Luck is not involved, only positive attitudes, focus and determination to win through. Sometimes the Chariot symbolizes new energy and willpower to win. 'A journey of a thousand miles starts with just one step' is appropriate for this card.

When signifying a person, the Chariot often represents a positive driving force in your life – someone who can motivate or inspire you to explore your own talents and abilities to the full. Such a person can act as a catalyst for beneficial changes and developments.

Finally, if other cards concur, the Chariot symbolizes news, visitors and activities associated with faraway places. Again, these events or contacts may encourage you to dig deep for the extra energy you need to complete a project, or to make important changes in your life.

Reversed Meaning

The Chariot reversed traditionally signifies envy, avarice and addiction. It also warns against the misuse of power, excessive pride and arrogance – in short, loss of self-containment and control. Pride may be reversed, turning into the kind of low self-esteem and lack of self-confidence that prevents many talented people from taking the first steps towards exploring their creative gifts. Wasting your personal resources through overwork, overwhelming ambition or through wilful neglect is the message here. You must think carefully about what you can do to get your own chariot back on the road again.

THE MAJOR ARCANA

VIII
JUSTICE

RULING SIGN
Libra

KEYWORDS
UPRIGHT: Logical decisions • Resolutions
REVERSED: Delays • Injustice

SWORD
represents truth and clarity, and symbolizes logical intellect expanded by intuitive responses and emotional honesty

SCALES
symbolize the subtlety and fine reasoning powers that Justice must exercise

FEMININE FIGURE
of Justice is a link with the ancient Egyptian goddess Maat who weighed the soul of the deceased against her feather of truth, and judged accordingly

Symbolism of the Card

THE ANCIENT SYMBOL OF JUSTICE AS A WOMAN WITH SCALES ORIGINATES WITH THE ANCIENT EGYPTIANS. THE EGYPTIAN GODDESS MAAT WEIGHED THE SOUL OF THE DECEASED AGAINST HER FEATHER OF TRUTH, AND JUDGED ACCORDING TO WHAT SHE FOUND.

This powerful idea found its way into many mythologies and religions, while female Justice remains an archetypal image we recognize all over the world today. The *feminine figure* of Justice on the tarot card delicately balances her *scales* on one finger, symbolizing the subtlety and fine reasoning powers that she must exercise. The scales themselves represent balance, harmony, objectivity and equality. They are the symbol of Libra, the astrological sign that is associated with this card.

The *sword* of Justice represents truth, clarity, and the ability to penetrate straight to the heart of the matter. It is the weapon of the intellectual warrior, cutting away all mental distractions. It is also the weapon of truth, defending reality against the alluring mists of illusion. In the hands of a feminine being, it symbolizes logical intellect expanded by intuitive responses and emotional honesty.

The combination of the sword and the receptive scales represents inner male and female principles. Both are needed if Justice is to be served, and both must be developed by the Fool on the journey of self-development signified by the tarot trumps as a whole. It is for this reason that Justice is paired with the elusive Hanged Man, who represents the sacrifices that must be made in the pursuit of an honest and truthful way of life.

Goddess of Reason

Justice, symbol of balance and fair play, is placed either at number eight, as in *The Renaissance Tarot*, or at number eleven in many modern decks. We chose the old position for two main reasons. First, this position means Justice is paired with the Hanged Man, representing the familiar tarot message of reason balanced by intuition, of balance and control united with dreams and freedom of spirit. And second, it places Strength at number eleven, where she introduces the inner, spiritual cycle of the tarot journey – following on from the first turning point, represented by the Wheel of Fortune.

Justice represents the embodiment of a praiseworthy characteristic – just as Faith, Hope and Charity were often depicted as semi-divine creatures of the imagination. Justice and her scales form an image that was familiar to the ancient Egyptians. The goddess Maat, whose name means 'truth and justice', weighed the souls of the dead against the Feather of Truth. Souls with a clear conscience would weigh exactly the same as the Feather. The soul was expected to recite the Negative Confession in the presence of the goddess, to show that he or she had lived a spiritual life. This confession bears a remarkable similarity to the biblical Ten Commandments. It includes the following statements: 'I have not robbed the poor ... I have made none to weep ... I have not inflicted pain ... I have allowed no man to suffer hunger ... I have not borne false witness ...'

The image of Justice became a powerful one, which was adopted by Christian art, along with the idea of scales weighing the souls of the dead. There is a painting of Justice in the Vatican, Rome, by Raphael which bears the Latin inscription *Ius suumcuique tribuit* – 'Justice gives each his due.'

An old belief connects this idea of heavenly rewards and retributions with the number eight. There were eight blessings for the chosen, and eight punishments awaiting the damned. And if you place the figure eight on its side, you get the infinity symbol – also associated with the cycles of karma, best understood as the law of cause and effect. What goes around, comes around, as we say thousands of years later. Fundamentally, this age-old belief in cosmic justice still prevails.

As a mature virtue, Justice appears between the Chariot and the thoughtful realm of the Hermit. In this position it signifies the passing nature of material success and the dangers of avarice. One of the statements in the Egyptian Negative Confession is: 'I have not increased my wealth except with such things as are my own possessions.' This shows that prosperity at others' expense was considered wrong thousands of years ago. The card Justice denotes equilibrium between the victories of the Chariot and the spiritual awareness of the Hermit. As always in the tarot trumps, striving for balance in the midst of duality must be accomplished if life is to be lived to the full and if the spirit is to flourish and develop.

Upright Meaning

Justice signifies the qualities of balance, order and clarity – and the need for these things. As a descriptive card of personality, Justice depicts someone who is fair, clear-thinking and balanced. Often these qualities are needed in professional life, and the card can represent those involved with the law, financial institutions, politics, unions and any organization that helps opposing sides to negotiate agreements. The card frequently appears in spreads connected with legal matters and other delicate negotiations. It is a fortunate symbol, indicating success in litigation and decisions in your favour – provided you are not being unreasonable in your demands. Justice is an unemotional card, and the decisions associated with it tend to be impartial.

Justice can denote a decision point in your life, a time when you must weight up the pros and cons of a situation and make a calm choice. Thinking logically about your decision may be difficult at first; Justice suggests that an impartial friend or adviser could help you to talk things through objectively before you come to any final conclusions.

Justice can suggest a marriage contract, especially when accompanied by the Hierophant, the Ace of Pentacles or the Ace of Cups. Otherwise, it does not signify marriage, although it may represent contracts relating to business partnerships.

Reversed Meaning

Justice reversed traditionally warns of delays in formal negotiations, and difficulties with legal or financial matters. Confusion surrounds any court cases, property negotiations or contract negotiations. You may also incur extra expenses connected with these matters, or find that things are not resolved in your favour.

Reversed Justice can be a card of divorce, sometimes accompanied by the Three of Swords or the Lovers reversed. However, it always refers to the legal and practical side of a parting – property settlements, financial agreements, the division of belongings and so on – rather than the more complex emotional issues that are involved.

IX
THE HERMIT

RULING SIGN
Virgo

KEYWORDS
UPRIGHT: Retreat • Wise guidance
REVERSED: Loneliness • Obstinacy

WHITE HEAD of the raven symbolizes the enlightenment and wisdom to be gained through what may be a challenging and lonely time

LANTERN illuminates the inside of the cloak to symbolize the inner world and foreshadow the journey through the underworld

STAVE connects the Hermit with the earth and symbolizes his inner strength and stability

RAVEN represents the alchemical progress of nigredo, which precedes all creative flowering and spiritual development

BARE TREE is the Tree of Life, stripped bare and waiting to put forth leaves and blossoms when the journey through the underworld has been completed

HOODED CLOAK symbolizes spiritual protection and shields the Hermit from the distractions of the outer world

Symbolism of the Card

SOLITARY AND SERIOUS, THE DETERMINED FIGURE OF THE HERMIT STRIKES A SOLEMN NOTE BETWEEN AIRY JUSTICE AND THE EXUBERANT WHEEL OF FORTUNE.

The Hermit's **hooded cloak** is a symbol of spiritual protection, shielding him from the outer world and all its glittering distractions. For, above all, this figure represents a retreat from the everyday into a private inner space. This message is amplified by the Hermit's **lantern**. Its rays of light illuminate the inside of the cloak, clearly symbolizing the inner world and foreshadowing the second, underworld, cycle of the tarot trumps to come.

The Hermit grasps a **stave** in his other hand. It connects him with the earth, with his path, and symbolizes his inner strength and stability. This stave is like a magician's wand, a conduit for the energies of the earth – this card is associated with the earth sign, Virgo, which is traditionally the sign of service. The Hermit serves as a quiet beacon, a wise and patient teacher who leads the traveller onward, offering silent support when it is needed. He marks out the path towards the gates of the underworld, a place with which he is extremely familiar.

A **bare winter tree** is growing in this twilight landscape. It is the Tree of Life, stripped bare, waiting to put forth leaves and blossoms once the sojourn in the underworld has been completed. Perched upon the branches is an alchemical figure, a white-headed **raven**. The raven signifies a process called the nigredo, or blackening, a stage of putrefaction, decay and darkness which was essential to the process. This stage has been identified by philosophers and mystics as representing the withdrawal of energy from outer concerns which precedes all creative flowering and spiritual development. This is a phase which is the Hermit's domain, a phase which lays the foundations for future events. The raven's **head** is white, symbolizing the enlightenment and wisdom to be gained through what may be a challenging and lonely time. It also signifies, like the Hermit's cloak, protection throughout the underworld journey.

The Wise Old Man

The Hermit, who symbolizes withdrawal from the world, is the last card before the first turning point of the tarot, signified by the Wheel of Fortune. Nine is also the last whole number, representing the culmination of a cycle. Ruled by Virgo, sign of service and solitude, the Hermit is a wise guide who beckons the Fool – leading him or her towards the inner worlds to come. As a symbolic figure he is variously the grandfather, sage, wizard and an elder magician or king. Solitary, rather than lonely, he has many correspondences with the mythic figure of Saturn and with the gate of darkness in alchemy, a process ruled by Saturn.

Florentine philosophers believed that the saturnine or melancholic mood was a fertile one. They saw it as an essential stage on the path to creative inspiration, self-knowledge and lightness of spirit. A contemporary psychiatrist might name it as pre-creative depression; a fairytale might envision it as the dark forest, laced with untrodden paths. Yet a wise old man or woman often lives amidst the trees, offering magical guidance to the lost child, questing knight, homeless princess or hopeful traveller. Saturn, in myth, was a grim figure. However, he was also the father of powerful Jupiter – leader of the gods and grandfather of shining Apollo, the sun god and creative spirit. The alchemists spoke of Apollo, a code name for gold, being born from the 'night of lead'. This dark process corresponded to putrefaction and decay, to night, to imprisonment and to a subsequent withdrawal from the world. But wrapped up within the layers of gloom lay a glistening golden stone – the wealth of creativity, vitality and spiritual clarity.

Hermits are found in numerous traditions and mystical practices. A period of contemplation, of isolation, is part of the stories of prophets, shamans, visionaries and sages. Solitary hermits lived in the wilderness, in caves, in the desert or hidden away in a forest. Many Eastern sages inhabited mountain caves, Renaissance magicians were advised to fast and spend time alone in retreat from the world before attempting their rituals.

By removing the stimulus of the world, the mind has a chance to hear itself, to reveal its dreams and to experience guidance without the distractions of everyday life. Spiritual retreat – often accompanied by fasting or purification of the body – is an ancient practice. Often, it accompanies a rite of passage – from childhood to maturity, from ignorance to wisdom, from one stage to the next. The Hermit of the tarot gathers his strength in silence, wrapping it around him like a cloak, in readiness for the next phase of development.

Upright Meaning

The Hermit represents a wise guide leading you towards an unknown future. This guide often appears as a teacher, therapist or inspirational friend. He or she is someone who is supportive, who

THE HERMIT

enables you to find your own way through a shadowy landscape. This card represents an extremely positive period in your life, when the foundations for your future are being constructed. However, you may not be able to see this clearly at the time, for it is only when you look back that you will see what was achieved by this period of withdrawal and inner change. You may feel very frustrated, especially if you are not used to musing upon events or thinking about your own feelings and reactions to things. You may gain little pleasure in the social events that you once enjoyed, preferring the company of a few close friends, or even wanting to be on your own for periods of time. Once these apparent limitations are accepted, however, you will be able to relax and find peace and contentment. The Hermit may be a solitary figure but he is not a lonely one.

When offering advice, by context or position, the Hermit counsels caution. This is not the time to share your thoughts, plans or decisions freely with others. Neither should you feel pressured into taking action before you feel ready. If you have an important decision to make now, simply bide your time. Your own intuition will guide you towards the right path but you may need to spend some time alone, or perhaps in some lovely unspoilt place, before you can be certain about what you need and want.

Reversed Meaning

You are in danger of ignoring wise advice or wasting your energy and resources in some way. You may be so busy filling up your time, your social calendar and your brain, that you are unable to be still and quiet. The Hermit reversed signifies a need to take stock, to slow down and to re-examine your goals and preoccupations. Sometimes, especially if there are reversed Cups in the same spread, this card symbolizes a lonely time when you are apparently unable to make satisfying friendships or relationships. You are simply changing direction, so do not panic, worry or despair. You will not be a hermit for ever, but only while you need a period of reflection and calm in your life.

THE MAJOR ARCANA

X

THE WHEEL OF FORTUNE

RULING PLANET
Jupiter

KEYWORDS
UPRIGHT: Destiny • Fortunate coincidence
REVERSED: Unexpected disruption

ANGEL
of Aquarius signifies the element of air and represents the winter – a time of hibernation

FIGURES
are bound to the wheel, representing the great wheel of fate and karma to which an individual soul is bound throughout life

BULL
of Taurus symbolizes the element of earth and represents the spring – a time of new growth

PHOENIX/EAGLE
of Scorpio symbolizes the element of water and represents the autumn – a time of gathering in the fruits of the earth

SNAKE
represents eternity, immortality and creation

LION
of Leo signifies the element of fire and represents the height of summer – a time of lush growth

STAR
is a symbol of completion and celestial powers weaving patterns beyond the reach of human beings

Symbolism of the Card

THE WHEEL OF FORTUNE, OR MINOR FORTUNE, STANDS AT THE FIRST TURNING POINT OF THE TAROT TRUMPS. IT IS ALWAYS IN MOTION.

The ups and downs of fortune are traditionally represented by the *figures* attached to the wheel. They are eternally experiencing the positive and negative events of every life. The idea of being bound to a wheel has oriental origins, representing the great wheel of fate and karma to which the individual soul is bound throughout his or her lifetime. The wheel is enclosed by a *snake* with its tail in its mouth.

This symbol is called the Ouroboros, and it represents creation, immortality and, eternity. Ouroboros was the name given to the serpentine king of magic by medieval hermetic philosophers and alchemists, who saw it as a symbol of the universe and of all creation. Here the Ouroboros embraces an eight-pointed *star*, a symbol of completion and celestial powers weaving patterns beyond the reach or understanding of human beings.

Creatures symbolic of the four fixed signs of the zodiac appear in the four corners of this card. These are, in zodiac order, the *Bull*, symbol of Taurus, and of the spring season when this sign appears in the northern hemisphere. It is symbolic of the element of earth, and of the physical senses. The *Lion* of Leo signifies the height of summer, August and harvest time. It is symbolic of the element of fire, of intuition and imagination. The *Phoenix or Eagle* of Scorpio represents the autumn, a time when the fruits of the earth are gathered in. In northern latitudes, this was traditionally a time of reflection on the passing year, and of planning for the year to come. Scorpio represents the element of water, the emotions and sexuality. The *Angel* of Aquarius represents the heart of the northern winter, January, when there is little light or warmth. It is a time of hibernation; storing energy for the fertile spring season. Aquarius signifies the powers of thought, and the element of air, last of the four elements of the ancient world that were believed to be the building blocks of all living things.

The Wheel of Fortune therefore represents life and its many cycles, which are continually manifesting on all levels – mental, physical, emotional and spiritual.

The Wheel Turns

The Wheel of Fortune is placed at number ten, a transcendent number signifying both the end of a cycle and new beginnings. As the Wheel turns, it opens the way for the second, spiritual, cycle of the tarot trumps. Prepared by experience for his initiation, the Fool now reaches a turning point because he is standing at the entrance to the unconscious underworld.

The Wheel of Fortune is traditionally surrounded by the four symbolic creatures of the fixed signs of the zodiac – Taurus the Bull, Leo the Lion, the Eagle or Phoenix of Scorpio and the Angel of Aquarius. In the northern hemisphere, these in turn correspond to the four seasons – spring, summer, autumn and winter. Many wheel symbols connected the wheel's quarters with the four directions and the four main winds of the earth. As a cyclical symbol, the Wheel represented the creation and evolution of the seven planets of classical astrology – Sun, Moon, Mercury, Venus, Mars, Jupiter and Saturn.

Jupiter is linked to the Wheel of Fortune, a planet loosely associated in astrology with good fortune. However, Jupiter can only bestow his abundance on those who have prepared the ground beforehand, recalling the biblical saying: 'As ye have sown, so shall ye reap.' This idea is closely allied with Eastern notions of karma, the setting in motion of causes which will, one day, have an effect in one's life, or the lives of one's children or grandchildren. Karma also applies to the belief in reincarnation – causes set up in past lives may wreak havoc or draw blessings in this one.

The Wheel of Fortune originates with ancient civilizations. The Etruscan goddess Vortumna – who evolved into Roman Fortuna – was called 'She who turns the Year'. The turning of the year, and all the years of life itself, was always associated with the mother goddesses who ruled birth, death and rebirth.

Medieval images often showed men riding on the Wheel of Fortune – rising up to riches and influence but falling again as the wheel turned, and becoming poor peasants. The Celtic Wheel belonged to another goddess, Arianrhod; it appeared in the night sky as the Milky Way, and was the path to rebirth and the magical paradise beyond earthly death. By the Middle Ages, the goddesses and their wheels were amalgamated into the figure of Dame Fortune, who still managed to appear in church windows, pagan figure though she was. The Wheel of Fortune is still a popular symbol today, while the goddess has become Lady Luck. As mandala and turning point of the tarot trumps, the Wheel turns, and the Fool tumbles into the underworld as part of his or her fortune.

Upright Meaning

The Wheel of Fortune brings a sparkling, expansive and impersonal energy into your life. It invariably represents change, movement and unexpected twists of fate. New places, new friends, surprising directions or ideas may all conspire to throw you off-course – wearing a large smile on your face. Events and experiences outside your personal control are signified, and nothing may turn out as you planned it. The great Roman philosopher, Ovid (43 BC–AD 17), wrote something that perfectly encapsulates the core meaning of this exciting card: 'Chance is always powerful. Let your hook be always cast, in the pool where you least expect it, there will be a fish.'

When the Wheel of Fortune describes an aspect of personality, it stands for an unsettling but exhilarating phase when you may be bursting with creative energy. The surrounding cards will show you how this energy may be channelled into your life, for it may relate to love, career or even a sudden change of home. The Wheel of Fortune alone simply means positive revolution, and often a simple lucky break that changes your life for the better. So assess the accompanying cards carefully, for this card, in itself, represents energy and expansion – and these may take one or several forms.

If the Wheel of Fortune describes an individual, it represents someone who will expand your life, your sense of yourself, or who will benefit you in many positive ways. If a love affair is suggested, it may not last for years – but it will free both you and your partner in some way. Any love relationship indicated by this card is a happy experience, and perhaps a fated encounter.

Reversed Meaning

As the Wheel of Fortune spins, it does not always bring you the result you desire. In the reversed position, this card signifies a bumpy ride, with a few challenging surprises along the way. Traditionally, the reversed Wheel is linked with harvesting the fruits of your past actions. Causes set in motion long ago will now bring about events, meetings and turns of fortune. These, in accordance with the impersonal nature of the Wheel of Fortune, may be life-enhancing or problematic. However, you may be sure that they are part of a much larger pattern, and as such are meaningful and important.

XI
STRENGTH

RULING SIGN
Leo

KEYWORDS
UPRIGHT: Unconditional love
REVERSED: Fear of failure

INFINITY SYMBOL
signifies the eternal love and strength of the goddess

MAIDEN
is an aspect of Sophia, or Wisdom, and of all tender-hearted mother goddesses in myth and legend

LION
links this card to its ruling sign, Leo

UNICORN
symbolizes everybody's animal nature and embodies both the masculine and feminine principles

FLOWERS
signify freshness, new life, springtime and hope

BLUE ROBES
of the maiden represent the sky, home of mother night and awesome inspiration to generations of ancient peoples

Symbolism of the Card

STRENGTH PRESENTS THE IMAGE OF A MAIDEN TAMING A UNICORN. THE THEME OF THIS CARD IS UNCONDITIONAL LOVE, WHICH IS SO STRONG THAT IT OVERCOMES ALL OBSTACLES AND HEALS ALL CONFLICTS.

A woman with a lion is, perhaps, the most familiar image for this card, although there are several variations, including a male figure. Such is the unconditional love of the goddess figure on Strength that it is strong enough to tame a wild and ferocious beast – the *unicorn*. The *maiden* on this card, in its original position at number eleven, represents yet another divine feminine figure within the scheme of the tarot trumps. She is an aspect of Sophia, or Wisdom, and an aspect of all tender-hearted mother goddesses in myth and legend. Her *blue robes* represent the sky, home of mother night and awesome inspiration to generations of ancient peoples. Above her head is the figure-of-eight *infinity symbol*, which traditionally appears on this card. It signifies the eternal love and strength of the goddess.

The unicorn himself symbolizes everybody's animal nature – the qualities of lust, rage and instinct that must be refined and tamed by a loving spirituality. As a symbol, unicorns embody both masculine and feminine principles, being associated with both the sun and moon. This animal was said to be incredibly fierce and impossible to catch. Only a maiden could ensnare him with her gentle charms. Meadow *flowers* flank the pair, signifying freshness, new life, springtime and hope. Above the picture, a *lion* appears to play among the flowers. This links the card to its astrological ruler, the sun, whose symbol is a lion. Leo is the zodiac sign associated with Strength, a sign which rules the heart, and which must find courage through love and a sense of creativity. The lion and the unicorn are traditional adversaries but are also inextricably paired as sun and moon, male and female, hot and cold – the eternal pairs of opposites which need one another to create a whole. Again, this echoes a favourite tarot theme. Here, love and courage are the catalysts for psychological and emotional union.

The Power of Love

The card of Strength traditionally depicts a woman opening a lion's mouth. Some later tarot decks even show a muscular male figure, others a woman breaking a stone pillar. For *The Renaissance Tarot* we have chosen to show a woman subduing a mythical unicorn, an image which resonates with the historical period and also with the secret symbolism of this complex card. Associated with the zodiac sign Leo, which rules the heart, Strength is a card of love and determination, self-discipline and triumph over unruly forces of all descriptions.

Strength, at number eleven, begins the second cycle of the tarot trumps. It represents many things. Fortitude (another name for this card) or strength in adversity was one of the classical virtues – Temperance and Judgement are the other virtues represented in the tarot. Strength is also sometimes known as the Enchantress. In fact, it represents both stoicism and faith springing from unconditional love and trust in a higher power. By subduing a fierce wild beast, the female figure is showing the triumph of love over aggressive instincts and the refining powers of the feminine – a recurring theme in medieval Courtly Love poetry, in Eastern Tantric philosophy and Mesopotamian myth. In this ancient tale, Inanna/Ishtar, the Mesopotamian goddess, gave her love to a wild and savage man. Through her love he became civilized, and led to the city gates to begin his new life. As an emblem of love's power, the unicorn was a favourite creature of artists, poets and storytellers for centuries.

The legend of the virgin and the unicorn seems peculiarly apt for Strength. A unicorn could only be tamed by a virgin maiden, often shown in an enclosed garden, symbolic of her inviolate state. In secular tales, love is victorious and succeeds in capturing or killing the unicorn, which represents unbridled lust and promiscuous passions.

In the *Bestiaire d'Amour*, written in the thirteenth century by Richard de Fournival, the unicorn is the lover and the maiden his beloved. Love is personified as the huntsman who cunningly beguiles the unicorn: '... But Love, the skilful huntsman, has set in my path a maiden in the odour of whose sweetness I have fallen asleep, and I die the death to which I was doomed.'

Medieval beast-taming virgins are closely related to their ancient goddess ancestors – especially Artemis, the fierce Greek virgin huntress, and Roman Diana. A lunar emblem, later linked to the Virgin Mary in art and fable, the unicorn came to symbolize love, betrothal, chastity, purity and strength. In the Book of Job (King James Bible, 1611) it says: 'Will the unicorn be willing to serve thee, or abide by thy crib? ... Wilt thou trust him, because his strength is great?' Strength, love and the desire to polish and refine our animal nature so that its vitality serves us are challenges signified by this card. Strength is followed by the sacrificial Hanged Man, and the true descent into the tarot's mystical underworld kingdom. This card suggests the qualities the Fool will

STRENGTH

require on this part of the journey. And just as the lovely, wild unicorn surrenders to the gentle maiden, so the Fool must surrender to love and strengthen his or her faith for the adventures that lie ahead.

Upright Meaning

Strength is a wonderful card to find in any spread, for it signifies the faith that can move mountains and the love that truly conquers all adversity. It can mean triumph and victory, but these spring from an optimistic frame of mind, self-love and faith in your own strengths. Your own positive vibrations will enable you to find a way through any apparent difficulties and will draw help and encouragement into your life when you most need them. Strength can represent a generous, vibrant person coming into your life. They may champion your cause, offer practical help or come to your aid in some way. This person is a loyal friend and fierce ally – you will benefit in many ways from knowing them.

The positive force of Strength suggests transformation through loving energies in whichever area of your life it describes. Career difficulties, disputes or conflicts can be overcome, disagreements between friends and neighbours healed, opposition dissolved. When referring to a personal relationship, Strength counsels reconciliation and acceptance. Love is still alive between you, whatever your differences. It is time to swallow your pride – so kiss and make up, and look forward to a happier future.

The love that exists between human beings and animals is also signified by Strength. Where appropriate, this card refers to such a bond, suggesting that the affection you feel for this creature will open your heart and allow love to flow more freely in your life.

Reversed Meaning

Strength reversed generally denotes fear, loss of hope and lack of courage. These feelings may overwhelm you personally or they might describe a situation in your life where you and others have simply given up the fight. Fear is the culprit here. But Strength, even in the reversed position, is telling you that you can overcome fear and, indeed, any enemy to your wellbeing. Progress and happiness are still possible, but you may have to fight quite a battle to win them.

XII
THE HANGED MAN

RULING PLANET
Neptune

KEYWORDS
UPRIGHT: Willing sacrifice • Waiting
REVERSED: Stop and think

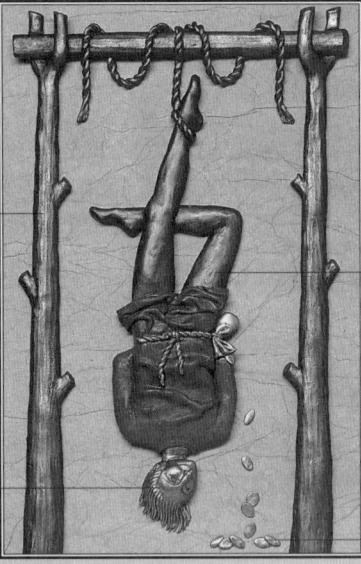

T-CROSS made from sturdy tree trunks links the Hanged Man with gods who were often sacrificed or turned into trees

SERENE FACE of the Hanged Man illustrates the card's inner meaning of willing sacrifice rather than death or punishment

LEGS in a figure-four position echo the traditional pose of the Emperor, suggesting that his solid world has been turned upside down by the descent into the underworld

COINS falling from the Hanged Man's pouch underline this card's message of sacrifice – he is entering a world where money is unimportant

Symbolism of the Card

PERHAPS THE MOST IMPORTANT SYMBOLIC FEATURE OF THE HANGED MAN IS HIS SERENE EXPRESSION. THIS, EXPERTS BELIEVE, IS INTENDED TO REVEAL THE CARD'S INNER MEANING OF WILLING SACRIFICE RATHER THAN DEATH OR PUNISHMENT.

The Hanged Man's *legs* are shown in the figure-four position, echoing the Emperor's traditional pose. This suggests that the solid world of the Emperor has been, quite literally, turned upside down by the descent into the underworld, or unconscious world of dreams, represented by the second cycle of the tarot trumps.

Coins fall to the ground from the Hanged Man's pouch, underlining the message of sacrifice. The Hanged Man is entering a world where money is unimportant, for money represents the outer world and the Hanged Man is deep in his explorations of the inner, spiritual and unconscious realms.

Traditionally, the figure of the Hanged Man is suspended from a tau- or *T-cross* made from sturdy tree trunks. This design links the figure with a number of legends of dying and resurrected gods, who were often sacrificed or turned into trees. At one time there were sacred groves all over Europe where the prevailing goddess and her sacrificial consort were venerated. The Hanged Man precedes number thirteen, Death, the ultimate underworld symbol. The motif of sacrifice, of turning away from the everyday world, has been built up since number nine, the Hermit. Now, the symbolism suggests, the point of preparation for major changes has been reached – ordinary concerns are suspended, just like the figure. And, just like the figure, there is no reason to be afraid because other treasures await on the other side of the abyss.

Symbolic Sacrifice

The sacrificial figure of the Hanged Man is placed at twelve, between the loving discipline of Strength and the inevitability of Death. Tarot images of the goddess aside, he is perhaps the most outstandingly pagan symbol in the entire deck – this is why his image puzzles, disturbs and fascinates anyone who first looks at a deck. The Hanged Man is undergoing a ritual sacrifice, for if he were to be executed he would be hanged by the neck – a widespread public practice for hundreds of years. Certainly, the creators of the original images were very familiar with the gallows. Medieval criminals were sometimes hanged upside down as a form of public humiliation, known as baffling. However, the image and practice has ancient roots – and was used by heretical secret societies in initiation rituals.

Odin, the powerful Nordic god, hung himself upside down on a tree 'for nine long nights'. As he sacrificed himself as an offering to himself, he was granted tremendous inspiration and wisdom because he gained the knowledge of the runes. Runes are an ancient alphabet and were used for divination purposes by rune-masters and -mistresses in northern Europe. Ritual sacrifices of god-kings in groves of trees were common all over ancient pagan Europe – originally, these sacrifices were real human beings but, later, effigies or animals were substituted.

The theme of dying, or becoming unconscious, and rising again is a widespread belief across numerous mythologies. During the Renaissance and later, this card was associated with Judas Iscariot, whose betrayal of Jesus led to his crucifixion. It was sometimes called the Thief or the Traitor. Judas acts as a dramatic catalyst in the biblical story, for his betrayal and its results are foreseen by Jesus, who is aware that he must die and in doing so effectively sacrifice himself to the greater power of God. This story, whether it is history or poignant symbolism, bears a striking resemblance to older myths of sacrifice and redemption.

No old pack depicts a Hanged Man with anything other than a serene expression. There can be little doubt that the figure is not supposed to represent pain, suffering or punishment. Curiously, the god Odin was not only a dying and resurrected deity: he was also a trickster god who could shape-shift, or change his shape at will. Trickster gods commonly rule over thieves, as well as language, magic and travelling. So, tenuous though the theory may be, there are well-established links between thieves, sacrifice and deities who entered the realms of death and were able to return to life. The Hanged Man is associated with the planet Neptune, which rules dreams, sacrifice, spiritual love, mysticism and inspiration. Significantly, it is also the planet of lies, confusion and betrayal. The perceptions of the Fool are now turned upside down; a new pattern will eventually emerge out of this cosmic kaleidoscope.

Upright Meaning

The Hanged Man is entirely at home in the world of dreams, where his upside-down way of looking at things makes perfect sense. Transfer him to the everyday world, however, and life may seem to be entering a strange and somewhat surreal phase. As, indeed, it is.

This card typifies those times when you simply have to let go, sacrifice your expectations and cultivate patience. As the tarot symbolizes a spiritual journey, so the Hanged Man symbolizes those moments in any journey where you must pause and wait for the next direction. Such times may appear to be unproductive to outsiders, for little happens, there is no news and time itself seems to stretch to infinity. Inside, underneath, things are happening in secret, out of sight and out of reach. You cannot take decisions now, or control events in love, work or any other practical direction. All you can do is acknowledge this pause, learn to relax, and understand that it will not last for ever.

You may be asked to give up something when this card appears.

The Hanged Man embodies the symbol of willing sacrifice. You may need to leave a relationship, a dead-end job, a mistaken course of education or a set of beliefs that no longer serve you. If you feel trapped by something in your life, that is what you must look at. Perhaps your expectations need changing, perhaps you need to sacrifice your ideas of what is normal and unearth the truth of what you really need. You are being given a breathing space in which to explore these things and make important discoveries for yourself.

Sometimes, when its position or other cards suggest this, the Hanged Man symbolizes a person who is mourning for something or someone. This is a necessary process that cannot be hurried, but there is hope and renewal at the end of it.

Reversed Meaning

The Hanged Man reversed warns against selfishness, emotional manipulation and thoughtless actions of every kind. Loss and reversals of fortune are suggested in a general sense – the reasons behind them are subtle and can sometimes be hard to understand. Lack of self-awareness and loss of contact with your intuition may cause you to make bad decisions, especially those involving investments and finances in general. Failure to see the larger picture is suggested, so do not take any irrevocable steps at this time. Wait for a better opportunity to act.

As a personal card, the reversed Hanged Man signifies some kind of martyr–victim scenario. One person oppresses the other, but both are locked into a destructive game that neither can win. The position will reveal whether you are pressuring someone or whether you are the victim of such emotional pressure yourself. Either way, it is time to let go, because this is entirely a no-win situation for all concerned.

XIII
DEATH

RULING SIGN
Scorpio

KEYWORDS
UPRIGHT: Transformation • Renewal
REVERSED: Stagnation • Lethargy

PHOENIX is both lunar and solar and is a powerful symbol of regeneration, death and rebirth

FLAMES of the phoenix's nest echo the alchemists' great work, which involves burning and reducing everything to ashes before the creation of alchemical gold

SKULL and crossbones act as a reminder that death, in the tarot trumps, is simply the end of an established order so as to make room for fresh experience

GRIFFINS link this card with the Chariot, as a card of time's greater cycles and mysterious patterns

Symbolism of the Card

THE CARD OF DEATH IS DOMINATED BY THE IMAGE OF A FIERY PHOENIX, SYMBOL OF REGENERATION, DEATH AND REBIRTH. IT DOES NOT SYMBOLIZE A LITERAL DEATH BUT A TRANSITIONAL STAGE OF ENDINGS AND BEGINNINGS – A REBIRTH.

The ancient Egyptians believed that at the point of death the soul assumed the form of a bird, flying free of the body. Many legends refer to the phoenix, which was said to weep precious incense because its blood was made from balsam, a sweetly scented gum resin burned as an offering all over the ancient world.

The *phoenix* is both lunar and solar. It dies in the *flames* of its own nest, and after three days regenerates itself and is reborn. It appeared on Roman cinerary urns containing the ashes of the dead and, later, on Christian tombs to symbolize everlasting life. As an alchemical symbol, the phoenix represents the great work, in which everything is burned and reduced to ashes before the elixir, or alchemical gold, is created.

The *skull* and crossbones on the tomb beneath the phoenix refer to the usual, grim, medieval image of a human skeleton shown on the card, calling forth everyone's fears of this inevitable human event. They also serve to remind us that death, in the tarot trumps, is simply a step along the way – the death of an established way of thinking, feeling or living, in order to make room for fresh experience.

Two *griffins* flank the skull and crossbones, linking this card with the Chariot, as a card of time's greater cycles and mysterious patterns which can often only be seen and understood with hindsight.

The Dark Moon

As implacable force and inevitable destination, Death appears at number thirteen – a number surrounded by superstition because it is a number associated with the lunar goddess. There are thirteen moon months, or lunations, in each year. The thirteenth cycle of the moon occurs during the northern hemisphere's winter months; if the year is taken to begin in March with the spring, as the pagan year always did, the last moon occurs in February – often a gloomy, icy month at the end of a long, hard winter. At this time of year, signs of new life are very few and far between, and the hours of daylight are short.

The traditional figure of Death – appearing in churches, in mystery plays, in art and in legend – is that of a human skeleton, carrying a scythe with which he cuts down the living. The acceptance of death as a natural event, as part of the cycle of life, is evident in every ancient religion. Symbolically, in the tarot as in numerous philosophies, Death represents transformation, initiation and offers the prospect of renewal and rebirth. Significantly, Death is followed by the angel of Temperance, which symbolizes restoration. Had it been intended to represent the end of life, it would have appeared at the end of the tarot trumps and not have been followed by eight more cards.

For *The Renaissance Tarot* we have chosen to show a phoenix, a mythical creature signifying death and rebirth. The phoenix is one of the symbolic creatures associated with the sign of Scorpio, which rules this card, as it is emblematic of the power to regenerate oneself. This wonderful creature is both lunar and solar. It is consumed by flames and lies dead for three days – just as the moon is dark for three days before the new moon appears in the sky. Rising from its own ashes on the third day, the phoenix becomes a glittering firebird once more – a glorious symbol of the sun. For the alchemists, the phoenix represented the red elixir of life, the lapis or goal of the process, alchemical gold and eternal wisdom.

Initiations – in ancient Egypt, Greek Eleusis and shamanistic rituals – always included an encounter with the Lord of the Abyss, Death. The presence of life as death's companion is symbolized in many cultures by dance and celebration – from the Mexican Day of the Dead to the Hindu god Siva who is lord of death and lord of the dance. Following on from the sacrifice of the Hanged Man, Death represents a willing surrender to the forces of nature – just as the mythic phoenix chose to die by burning itself in a nest of flames. That a new self emerges from the underworld, from the consuming flames and from every descent, is the profound and powerful message of this card.

Upright Meaning

Number thirteen, the tarot trump called Death, cannot help but evoke fearful reactions in both the inexperienced reader and the anxious enquirer. In redesigning this card, we hope some of these superstitious fears will be soothed, and that the true meaning of this powerful card may shine through. For, just as the phoenix symbolizes resurrection and renewal, so Death signifies that a potent transformative experience lies ahead for you. The approach to this important time in your life may take several forms. Most commonly, there are endings and unfinished business to deal with – particularly in your emotional world. However, creative projects or lengthy periods of work towards a personal goal may also be ending, leaving you empty for a time. Your life may seem to come to a temporary halt, there is a sense of suspended animation as if the world is holding its breath. In the legend of the phoenix, this phase resembles the three days before it emerges, reborn, from the ashes of its nest of spices. During this phase you may reassess your goals, relationships or anything else that is important to you – but you may find it difficult to take constructive action for a time.

When signifying a relationship, Death represents intense, life-changing connections that are like no other you have ever experienced. Your ideas about love and intimacy may be altered for ever, you may know depths of passion you are unprepared for. It is crucial to look very thoughtfully at the surrounding cards, to see the details and understand the implications of this strong and irresistible attraction. If you are already involved, this card may signify the ending of a long-term relationship, or the end of a phase within it – perhaps through the birth of a child, a commitment to make it work after a difficult patch, or a dramatic change in personal circumstances such as a move to another country.

There can be no doubt that Death is a serious card, signifying an intense and dramatic time. But its energy is life-enhancing, vital and ultimately transformative.

Reversed Meaning

A period of stagnation, inertia and possibly depression is signified by Death reversed. It is as if there is a thick veil between you and your world, preventing you from experiencing life to the full. Something inside you is resisting change or is unwilling to let go and move on. When you discover what this is – perhaps a relationship, job or way of life – you can begin to relax and overcome your fears. A new chapter of your life is about to unfold if you simply take the first step.

XIV
TEMPERANCE

RULING SIGN
Sagittarius

KEYWORDS
UPRIGHT: Adaptability • Harmony
REVERSED: Imbalance • Restlessness

BLACK WING
represents night, earth, structure and stillness

WHITE LIQUID
represents water, receptivity, assimilation and the feminine principle

BLENDING FLUIDS
shows that the masculine and feminine energies must be balanced and blended within an individual, a relationship and within life itself if harmony is to prevail

RED WING
of the angel symbolizes the 'reddening' stage of alchemy when the process gains life and energy after a period of withdrawal

RED LIQUID
represents fire, action, heat and the male principle

FLOWING WATER
represents the flow of time and the importance of fluid connections between hearts and minds

TEMPERANCE

Symbolism of the Card

THE FEMININE FIGURE OF TEMPERANCE IS PRESENTED AS AN ALCHEMICAL ANGEL, BLENDING LIQUIDS BETWEEN TWO VESSELS. SHE REPRESENTS A CLASSICAL VIRTUE, EXTOLLING MODERATION IN ALL THINGS IN ORDER TO ACHIEVE A BALANCE.

The symbol of *blending fluids* also refers to the other meaning of the card, which springs from its Latin root, *temperare*, meaning 'to blend, moderate and harmonize opposing factors'. We have chosen to show the fluids as red and white liquids. These are alchemical symbols – the *red liquid* represents fire, action, heat and the male principle. The *white liquid* represents water, receptivity, assimilation and the feminine principle. These energies must be balanced and blended within an individual person, within a relationship and within life itself if harmony is to prevail. Temperance is linked to the Lovers, for it represents the higher levels of blending energy which must enter into a true union between lovers, or within the mind, body and spirit of an individual.

The angel's wings are red and black, showing again the alchemical symbolism of this card. The *black wing* represents the night, earth, structure and stillness. The *red wing* symbolizes the rebirth, the 'reddening' stage of alchemy when the process gains life and energy after a period of withdrawal and enclosure. Again, the message is that both qualities are needed for transformation, both qualities have an important part to play in every story as it unfolds. The wings link this figure with the element of air. The liquids represent water, the use of red symbolizes fire, and the figure stands on the earth – connecting all four ancient elements with the central concept of balance and harmony. This motif is emphasized by the four sections of the angel's robe; all four ingredients are necessary to complete the whole.

The *flowing water* surrounding Temperance represents the flow of time, and the fluid connections between hearts and minds which characterize the most rewarding relationships in our lives.

Alchemical Angel

The peaceful figure of the Angel of Temperance stands at number fourteen, between the darkness of Death and the outrageous energies of the Devil. Fourteen is a lunar number, representing the midpoint of the moon's twenty-eight-day cycle. In ancient Assyria, this day – along with the seventh and twenty-first, was marked by special rituals in honour of their goddess. The number fourteen is associated with energy, sexuality and the process of continuous change.

Temperance, or moderation in all things, was one of the classical virtues. Some old tarot packs revealed a sense of humour when they renamed this figure Intemperance, depicting an intoxicated woman gazing drunkenly out from the card. However, the root of the word 'temperance' is Latin, *temperare*, and means 'to moderate, to blend, to mix evenly'. The Angel of Temperance is always shown mixing liquids between two vessels – blending male and female, active and receptive, conscious and unconscious energies. The image and its title may be the kind of visual pun so popular during the medieval and Renaissance periods – the virtue of moderation is achieved by blending all things harmoniously. So the card successfully presents a dual message in name and symbol.

The Angel of Temperance is linked with the Lovers in the cycle of the tarot, amplifying the alchemical and sexual symbolism that is present in both cards. The balancing of male and female essence and energy was a popular alchemical motif – the fiery, red, male force blending with the cool, white, female waters to create gold, the symbol of wisdom and wholeness. Such imagery is found in Eastern Tantric teachings where even foods are classified according to their perceived energy and actions on the body. Red foods include meat, spices and alcohol; white foods include milk, fruit and vegetables.

Heating and cooling are both recurring processes in alchemy and must be performed several times, according to the old texts. Such ideas accord well with Temperance, who is eternally mixing the waters of life in a process which is erotic, medicinal, alchemical and philosophical. Since she appears in the second cycle of the tarot, she seems to be advising the Lovers on how to achieve perfect union on all levels.

This card is linked with the sign of Sagittarius, traditionally shown as a centaur. These mythical creatures, half-human, half-horse, symbolize the blending of animal instincts with human characteristics. Sagittarius is a mutable sign, which means it is constantly seeking a balance between active and receptive forces. Sagittarius is associated with philosophy. Temperance shows the Fool how to blend and balance his or her newly discovered ideas and beliefs into a cohesive philosophy and spiritual faith.

TEMPERANCE

Upright Meaning

Temperance symbolizes balance when it appears in a reading. It is a spiritual card, primarily concerned with feelings and states of mind rather than events or actions. It will be possible to restore harmony in any situation where arguments or disputes have occurred. This meaning applies whether the conflict is connected with your working life or has arisen with a partner or friend. You are able to act as a mediator, for your central feeling of calm well-being is powerful, and enables you to understand the differences between people without taking sides. You can see another person's point of view very clearly now, and do not feel threatened or disturbed by it. Resolving any difficult personal situation is simple at the moment, for it is the right time to create peace and settle disputes.

When describing your working life, Temperance also suggests renewed creativity and inspiration. New ways of working together, new approaches to creative dilemmas, fresh and original ideas – all these may enhance your days and lead to steady progress in the weeks and months ahead.

Reversed Meaning

Imbalance and disharmony are affecting you, your life or your relationships at this time. Traditionally, Temperance reversed signifies quarrels, competition with others and a restless atmosphere. It is also a warning against trying to do too much. If you are scattering your energies in too many different directions, you will achieve very little in the end. The presence of the Seven of Cups would underline this particular meaning, or perhaps the Five of Wands. It is not the right time to make any important decisions, for it is impossible to see any situation clearly at the moment. Imbalance in personal relationships is sometimes denoted. You or your partner may be feeling restless and frustrated, and unable to devote time or energy to your relationship. There could be sudden arguments or a great deal of suppressed tension between you. Look for ways to restore harmony, because Temperance does not indicate insoluble problems – merely a temporary incompatibility.

XV
THE DEVIL

RULING SIGN
Capricorn

KEYWORDS
UPRIGHT: Material power • Obsessive desires • Passion
REVERSED: Misuse of power

VINE LEAVES link the figure of the Green Man with Dionysus, god of the vine, and with life, ecstasy and the world of the senses

GREEN MAN is a powerful fertility icon with legendary links to the ancient gods of nature, especially Pan and Dionysus

TWIN MUSHROOMS represent the phallic powers of the Green Man and hint at his shamanistic inheritance

HOOVES of the Green Man signify his contact with magical animal spirits and amplifies the life-force present in this symbol

Symbolism of the Card

THE DEVIL IS PRESENTED AS A GREEN MAN, A FERTILITY ICON WITH LEGENDARY LINKS TO THE ANCIENT GODS OF NATURE – IN PARTICULAR, PAN AND DIONYSUS.

Green Men were carved in church decorations all over Europe, perhaps by pagan stonemasons, perhaps in acknowledgement of thousands of years of belief in such virile nature spirits. The conventional horned devil of medieval art represents the ancient horned gods of Europe, and was an attempt to personify him as evil and dangerous. In fact, he resembles classical sculptures of the Greek god Pan, and even more ancient depictions of shamans who often wore animal horns during ceremonial rituals that were designed to contact the animal spirits. This *Green Man* has been given *hooves* to signify his contact with such earthy magical figures and to amplify the life-force present in this symbol. The card of the Devil represents the tangible world of our five senses, which are neither subjective nor objective.

The *twin mushrooms* at the base of each leafy column represent the phallic powers of the Green Man and are another hint of his shamanistic inheritance – hallucinatory mushrooms were often used by northern shamans to induce mystical trance states. In Chinese symbolism, fungi are the food of the immortals and signify happiness and long life. The fecundity and strength of this card belongs to the earth itself, like the leaves and plants depicted on the image.

The figure is framed by *vine leaves*, linking it with Dionysus, god of the vine, and again with life, ecstasy and the empire of the senses.

The Green Man

For *The Renaissance Tarot* we have chosen to dispense with Christian imagery altogether, and we unveil the fifteenth tarot trump in his original, pagan form as an unruly, vibrant spirit of the natural world.

The European Devil is both the horned god of pagan Europe and the Green Man whose image appears in churches, and in folklore and legend. These two figures have separate identities – the horned god is a shamanistic hunter while the Green Man is a vegetation deity sacrificed annually to ensure fertility. Both figures are found all over Europe, in ancient Mesopotamia (now the Middle East) and elsewhere. Both are associated with seasonal rhythms, are inextricably linked with nature and, ultimately, with the great goddess. Both deities became confused with one another, and both took on sinister aspects when Christianity first assimilated and later demonized them.

The archetypal Devil is actually a composite figure, with elements of many of the old nature spirits and gods, including Pan, Dionysus, Jupiter, Pluto, Adonis and Celtic Cernunnos. The horned god and the Green Man are so ancient that their exact origins are now lost. The foliate heads of Green Men, and occasionally Women, gaze down from columns and friezes in churches all over Europe. Some sources suggest they were carved by Gnostics, secret pagans or heretics in a subversive act of defiance. Whatever the reason, there is no denying their curious presence. The Green Man, potent nature spirit, takes many forms – in Shakespeare's *A Midsummer Night's Dream* he is the mischievous spirit, Puck; in English folklore he is Robin Hood, dressed all in green and living in a forest with Maid Marian – his consort and the goddess in her guise as the May Queen, or maiden bride of spring. He is a potent earth spirit, and he corresponds to shamans, so-called witch-doctors and medicine men who embodied the ageless forces he symbolizes. He is energy made manifest in the material world, and he closely corresponds with the underworld deities who possessed great treasures and ruled over the spirits of the dead.

As the counterpart of the tarot's Hierophant or Pope, the Devil is the spiritual ruler of the material world – just as the Hierophant is the material, or earthly, ruler of the spiritual kingdom. In alchemy he corresponds to the Black Sun, counterpart of the Bright Sun – as night and day, body and soul. Each needs and is part of the other.

The Fool, as initiate, encounters the lord or king of the underworld when he seeks the twin treasures of wisdom and enlightenment. Learning to be in the material world, but not consumed or obsessed by it, is the symbolic message that is carried by this complex image.

Upright Meaning

The Devil, like Death, is another card that may cause a sharp intake of breath when he appears in a spread. Again, we have redesigned the card in the hope of quelling this reaction and revealing the inner meaning of the card which, quite simply, represents the material world. As the ultimate symbol of matter, the Devil can be interpreted in a number of different ways, so the context in which he appears in the reading is very important.

Money, possessions and your attitudes towards such things may be highlighted now. You may need to earn more money, or to be less inhibited about spending it. You may feel that you have denied yourself small luxuries or comforts for too long, and feel compelled to indulge yourself. A more expansive approach to your finances is generally a positive move, expanding you in other ways. If there is a significant number of Swords in the whole spread, beware of obsessive greed or of focusing exclusively on your material life.

When symbolizing a person, the Devil can denote someone who tries to buy your love or attention. He can also represent someone who values money and security above freedom and self-expression and who is, therefore, in a prison of their own making. Someone who is ruled by money, or the lack of it, is trapped in the world of matter that this card represents. Their creative, emotional and spiritual life suffers.

As a card of love or attraction, the Devil is the ambassador of desire. Like Dionysus, he embodies the unruly forces of lust, ecstasy and sexual obsession. There is intense erotic power in any encounter signified by this card, but love may be lacking. You may be consumed by this passion, or find yourself desired in this way. Such a union may not be able to sustain itself or to settle down into a more domestic partnership. But there is no denying its potency, nor its potential for changing your life.

Reversed Meaning

The Devil reversed signifies the abuse of power. This may be financial, personal, sexual or creative. As a career card, it suggests a desire for power, money and status which may be obsessive. The needs of others are ignored in the pursuit of visible success, creating relationship problems and difficulties with colleagues. When describing another person in your life, it refers to someone like this, someone you may be unable to communicate with because they are so consumed by their own desires.

As a relationship card, it describes an intense, inexplicable relationship which – although you may be aware of its dangers – you are unable to leave. You are bound to this person for good or ill. It is as if you are under a spell. Other cards will reveal the outcome of this relationship. Former associations are sometimes signified, too – but only where one person is still obsessed by the other and unable to let go. Emotional manipulation, blackmail or attempts to restart the relationship may cause you heartache.

As a predictive relationship card, the Devil reversed is similar to its upright meaning. It signifies unbounded sexual chemistry, mutual fantasies and an unusual level of obsession with one another. This may be short-lived but it can be wildly magnetic while it lasts.

XVI
THE TOWER

RULING PLANET
Mars

KEYWORDS
UPRIGHT: Sudden change • Drama
REVERSED: Chaos • Freedom

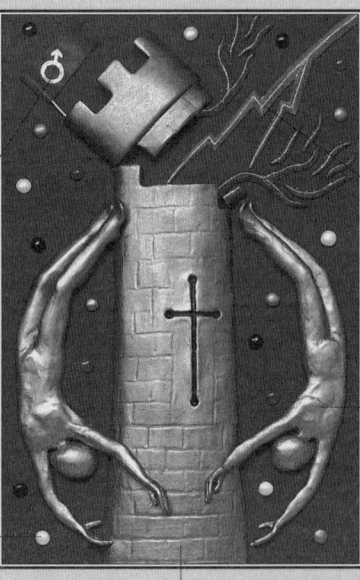

FLAG
flying from the top of the tower bears the symbol for Mars, ruling planet of the Tower card

DOTS
in the background symbolize the seeds of both past and future – the actions of the past have led to this moment of revolution

LIGHTNING
has knocked off the top of the tower's turret, thereby demonstrating the dangers of complacency

TWO FIGURES
fall from the tower, symbolizing liberation from the prison of structure and stale ideas

TOWER
is an intensely masculine symbol, signifying structure, material achievements and the world of matter

Symbolism of the Card

THE TOWER FOLLOWS THE DEVIL IN THE TAROT TRUMPS, REPRESENTING THE DRAMATIC UPHEAVAL THAT FOLLOWS AN ENCOUNTER WITH THE FORCES OF INSTINCT AND ANARCHY.

The *tower* itself is an intensely masculine symbol. It signifies structure, material achievements, the world of matter which seems to be indestructible. The tower is being struck by *lightning*, destroying the top of the turret and vividly demonstrating the dangers of complacency. Lightning is an attribute of all sky gods. In its negative sense it signifies destruction, power, rage and vengeance. In its positive sense, it symbolizes inspiration, fertility and the great surges of celestial energy that bring life-giving rain to the parched and barren earth.

A *flag* flies from the top of the tower, bearing the symbol for the planet Mars. This planet is linked with the Tower because it signifies assertive behaviour, energy, action and anger. Mars is the Roman name for the god of war, whose mythology grew from the Greeks' Ares – a god who protected animals and crops from storms, droughts and pestilence. Gradually, his protective qualities assumed a more aggressive nature until he became a battle god and the lover of Venus, goddess of love and beauty. Similarly, while the Tower may represent upheavals, it also signifies the need for change and growth. These may be achieved by dramatic means.

Two figures fall from the tower, echoing the figures on the Wheel of Fortune. They can symbolize the builders of the tower, suggesting a warning against identifying too closely with one's worldly achievements and becoming vain and arrogant. This image illustrates the old dictum, 'Pride goes before a fall.' And, like the lightning, the figures have a positive message, too. They symbolize liberation from the prison of structure and stale ideas.

The *dots* or small circles in the background symbolize the seeds of both past and future. The actions of the past have led to this moment of revolution, while the seeds of the future wait to be discovered.

Spirit of Revolution

The Tower is sometimes named the Tower Struck by Lightning, or the House of God. It is an apocalyptic image, which some scholars associate with the fall of the Holy Roman Empire – the most powerful organization in Renaissance Europe. Because it is connected with the Emperor, it seems to suggest the downfall of one used to wielding earthly power. Gnostic sects of the time certainly believed that the established Christian Church would be destroyed, and if their beliefs are connected with the creation of the tarot then this theory would make perfect sense. However, as with much Renaissance symbolism, and with the tarot in particular, the intended message of this card seems to be more complex than a simple religious–political prophesy.

Many tarot traditions link this image with the story of the Tower of Babel. This ill-fated structure was built by vengeful people, intent on reaching God's domain and exacting revenge for the Flood. God destroyed their attempt with a lightning bolt and cursed the builders. Thereafter, they all spoke in different languages and could not understand one another. The resulting confusion was a babble, or babel, of conflicting voices. As a symbol of downfall or reversals of fortune, the Tower is often considered to be a card of ill omen, and therefore can cause unease when it appears in a spread. However, it has many other layers of meaning and interpretation, which are linked to older myths.

Lightning has long been an attribute of the father gods of mythology – something that the Emperor also represents. It is seen as a destructive, vengeful force; yet it is also symbolic of enlightenment – the 'bolt from the blue', the flash of inspiration, the sudden moment of illumination. It is phallic, potent, creative and exciting, and as such it symbolizes masculine power. Shamans believed that a person struck by lightning was blessed – if they survived. Such a person was an immediate initiate, for lightning in all cultures is viewed as a divine act of cosmic power.

Lightning became associated with Lucifer, the fallen angel of the Bible, and hence with the Devil, who was said to attack Christians by hurling lightning bolts at their church towers. Hindu Siva's death-dealing third eye was credited with the same destructive powers, but it was also emblematic of the positive forces of creation and creativity.

These links between destruction and creativity are emphasized throughout the tarot. The Tower follows the Devil, a potent, earthy card – and is followed in turn by the Star, a gentle card depicting a goddess and her healing waters. This mysterious card might suggest the destruction of a masculine empire, followed by a return to the feminine values encapsulated in the Star. Certainly, the Tower is an underworld edifice, symbolizing the dangers of fixed attitudes or mental rigidity. These, the image suggests, are easily destroyed – and must be destroyed if growth and progress are to be achieved. The planet associated with the Tower is Mars, the planet of anger and creative drive, of energy and destructive impulses – much like the card itself.

THE TOWER

Upright Meaning

The Tower represents a dramatic liberation and awakening. Traditionally, destructive events and upheavals were signified by this powerful image. But such events are sometimes necessary, for, like the storm depicted on the card, they clear the air and refresh the spirit. As Thomas Fuller wrote in the seventeenth century: 'Security is the mother of danger and the grandmother of destruction.' When the Tower appears in a reading it often reveals a deep inner need for change which has long been suppressed. And so it seems to erupt into your life from nowhere, but like a distant storm it has been brewing and gathering energy for a long time. When the Tower describes you, or someone in your life, it signifies a period of intense inner change. During this time you may reject your old beliefs, behaviour patterns and values in favour of something new and different. You may discover anger for the first time, and experience intense moments of rage over past events and choices. Although this can be alarming, it will also free you from the past and allow you to develop and create a new life.

When answering a career query, the Tower frequently suggests redundancy or company collapse. It can also signify a career change that shocks others, for you could be inspired to retrain or earn your living in an unexpected fashion. Decisions and events linked to this card are always apparently sudden, changing the habits and routines of a lifetime overnight. It is important to realize that such changes are invariably positive, too. What has limited or stifled you is being cleared away, freeing the blocks to your creativity and spontaneity.

Reversed Meaning

Traditionally, the Tower reversed is associated with imprisonment. Sometimes this meaning is literally true, signifying some kind of prison, hospital or confinement. Most often, it is symbolic. A prison can be created within a stagnant relationship, dead-end job or limiting set of beliefs about yourself and your abilities. You will know if this interpretation is true for you. The reversed Tower also signifies intense revolution and disruption to your everyday routine. Losing your job, breaking up with your steady partner, having to leave your home suddenly – any of these events may occur now, in which case other cards will define the areas of change more clearly. But, however difficult these changes seem, they must be viewed in a positive light because they are ultimately a liberating and enlightening force in your life.

XVII
THE STAR

RULING SIGN
Aquarius

KEYWORDS
UPRIGHT: Hope • Faith • Healing
REVERSED: Pessimism • Tension

SEVEN STARS symbolize the seven sisters who featured in many myths from the ancient world

EIGHTH STAR emphasizes the title of this card and the woman's role as a goddess figure

WATER being poured from the cups symbolizes love, fertility, cleansing, healing and the elixir of life everlasting

NAKED WOMAN is reminiscent of classical images of Venus/Aphrodite, goddess of love

Symbolism of the Card

THE CENTRAL FIGURE IN THE STAR IS A NAKED WOMAN – THE GODDESS REPRESENTED IN THE EMPRESS IS REVEALED HERE, IN HER HIDDEN SPIRITUAL HOME.

A *naked woman* with stars is reminiscent of classical images of Venus/Aphrodite, goddess of love. Renaissance painters liked to depict Venus naked, most famously in Botticelli's lyrical painting of the birth of this goddess from a shell in the foaming ocean.

The *seven small stars* on this card hint at a mystical message, because seven was considered to be a particularly magical number in the medieval world. Shrines of Sophia, the Gnostic goddess of wisdom, were said to be protected by seven pillars designed to look like women. Seven sisters, a name we still use for the stars called the Pleiades, cropped up all over the ancient world – in Egypt as the seven goddesses who represented the seven stages of the afterlife; in Greece as the seven companions of Aphrodite, the goddess of love; in legend as seven prophetic priestesses who created the famous oracles of classical antiquity, such as the one at Delphi in Greece.

The *eighth star* is always shown above the woman's head, emphasizing the title of the card and the woman's role as a goddess figure. The woman pours *water* from two cups or vessels, symbolizing cleansing, fertility, abundance and the washing away of any suffering. These attributes also serve to link the card with the Empress although, with the Star, they usually refer to spiritual fertility and abundance. Water is also a profoundly feminine element in symbolism, emblematic of love, healing and the elixir of life everlasting.

Queen of Heaven

The Star pours her healing waters on to land and sea. She follows the dramatic image of the Tower and prepares the initiate for the kingdom of the lunar goddess, symbolized by the Moon. The Star is paired with the Empress, and represents the goddess unveiled in all her glory. As the Empress is often shown with a crown of stars, so the Star itself is the embodiment of all queens of heaven in many mythologies.

Venus/Aphrodite, goddess of love, peace, beauty and art, was known as the Morning and Evening Star, a title that the planet still bears today because it is the first star to be visible in the sky at twilight. Mesopotamian Ishtar/Inanna is, in many respects, the forerunner of

Venus/Aphrodite. She was praised in Babylonian prayers for being the goddess of the morning and the evening, the light of the world and the light of heaven.

In the *Epic of Creation*, one of the earliest epic poems ever preserved, Ishtar makes a perilous descent into the underworld to rescue her lover, the shepherd Dumuzi. At each of the seven gateways into death's kingdom she is forced to shed one of her garments or ornaments until, arriving in the place of the dead, she is naked. This is the origin of the Dance of the Seven Veils – originally the seven garments of the goddess. At her descent the earth becomes barren, just as the descent of Greek Demeter in search of her daughter causes the first winter to come to the earth. Once in the underworld Ishtar undergoes a terrifying ordeal at the hands of her dark sister, Erishkigal, queen of hell. The ritual form of the descent lasted three days in the Mesopotamian ceremony, at the end of which the goddess returned triumphant with her precious lover who was restored to life. This was an occasion of great rejoicing, with much music and dancing. The Star in the tarot trumps is very much a symbol of hope and life, placed firmly in the underworld but offering confirmation of life renewed.

Stars represent eternal hope, guidance and are also an attribute of Egyptian Isis, another queen of heaven whose worship continued for thousands of years, not only in Egypt but in Roman Italy, Greece and even France. The seven stars on this card may refer to the Pleiades, or Seven Sisters, which rise in May. The spring season is always associated with the Empress, as fertility goddess. The Romans called the Pleiades Virgins of Spring, while the Greeks linked them to Aphrodite. The larger star on the card is found in alchemical pictures as a symbol of completion and achievement. Many interpreters consider it to be an emblem of transcendence. The Fool has undergone many trials during his journey and is now able to rise above the petty concerns of the ego with true faith and trust.

The Star is associated with the zodiac sign of Aquarius, the water bearer. Its traditional astrological house is the eleventh, which presides over future hopes and wishes, amongst other things. It is also the house of love received, something this card is often taken to mean.

Upright Meaning

As a shining symbol of hope and renewal, the Star gleams in the darkness of the underworld. It is a symbol of spiritual energy and therefore brings harmony, protection, healing and inspiration. This, then, is its most important interpretation in a reading. The feelings

THE STAR

associated with the Star are intense but subtle, and may not manifest in the material world at all – instead, they make themselves felt in a mood of fresh vitality or in a strong but inexplicable sense of well-being.

When reading this card in a practical context, the beautiful spiritual vibrations of the Star must be taken into account. Do not look for spectacular events, but focus instead upon the inner world. Many metaphysical teachers assert that our inner attitudes and beliefs create energy, and colour our life experiences. So it is with this card – hope restored, a more positive outlook, renewed energy – all these things can contribute to improved circumstances in your work, relationships and self-expression.

Unexpected help is one of the traditional interpretations of the Star. This may come from private inspiration, through a book, workshop, lecture or friend – or represent a fortunate encounter, job offer or surprising turn of events. According to the type of spread and the nature of the reading, you may be inspired to offer much-needed practical help to another person. Healing energies find many channels – and practical help in painting a room, looking after a child or cooking a delicious meal can be just as restorative as a more esoteric 'healing' session. Above all, shared affection and laughter contribute to the uplifting moods suggested by this card.

Where appropriate, by position and context, the Star signifies the healing beauties of nature. It may prompt you to take a trip to some unspoilt place, or suggest that even a walk in the park could enhance your everyday life. Contact with animals, plants and the changing sky is so often lost amidst the pressures and stress of a busy life. The Star indicates that here is something you can enjoy if you choose.

Reversed Meaning

Reversed, the Star means loss of hope, disappointment and possibly depression. Frequently, it signifies exhaustion – whether mental, physical or emotional. When this is the case it may be accompanied by the Four of Swords, or appear with a number of reversed cards to suggest a general slowing-down. Deep down, optimism and hope remain – the gloomy mood indicated here is only temporary and superficial.

When describing a relationship, the Star reversed focuses on lack of trust, tension and sexual difficulties within a relationship. Spontaneity, fun and playful interludes are missing; one or both partners is unable to communicate freely and the relationship has a stiff, lifeless atmosphere. Overwork and personal doubts are the usual suspects – a short trip could be the first step towards resolving any problems.

THE MAJOR ARCANA

XVIII
THE MOON

RULING SIGN
Pisces

KEYWORDS
UPRIGHT: Dreams • Visions • Illusions
REVERSED: Confusion • Insincerity

MOON
is shown with the new moon inside the full moon to show that they are part of an endless cycle

TWO TOWERS
represent the gateway into the moon's mystical kingdom

TWO DOGS
have links with many mythological figures and defend the boundaries between waking and sleeping, the physical and spiritual realms

CRAYFISH
symbolizes the borders between dreams and the unconscious and physical reality

POOL
is the gateway to the moon, which represents intuitive feminine wisdom

Symbolism of the Card

THE MOON IS CONNECTED TO DREAMS AND THE UNCONSCIOUS, WHICH WILL OFTEN SEND INTUITIVE MESSAGES TO THE WAKING MIND VIA DREAMS, ESPECIALLY WHEN A NEW DEVELOPMENT IS IMMINENT.

The *moon* herself is shown with the slender crescent of a new moon inside the complete circle of the full moon. This symbolizes beginnings and completion, suggesting they are an endless cycle – for no sooner has one chapter ended than another must begin.

The *two towers* signify the gateway into the moon's mystical kingdom, just as turreted gatehouses were often built at the entrances to medieval cities. In art and legend, towers are often the home or prison of virgins and beautiful maidens such as Rapunzel. Sleeping Beauty pricked her finger in a tower room and fell asleep, imprisoned in the land of dreams. These untouchable women have strong links with the High Priestess, as one-in-herself – a self-contained aspect of the goddess whose domain, the moon, is revealed on this card. As guardian creatures of the realms of the underworld, the *two dogs* are linked with the Greek moon goddess Hecate; with Egyptian Anubis, god of the dead; with Hades and Pluto (king of the underworld); and with the virgin huntresses of myth, such as Roman Diana – another moon goddess. They defend the boundaries between waking and sleeping, the known and the unknown, the physical and spiritual realms.

The *pool* we see at the base of this card symbolizes the element of water, perhaps the most feminine element of all, and often linked with the moon which controls the tides of the earth's oceans. Water has many sacred attributes – cleansing, fertilizing water is symbolic of life in many mythologies. In Celtic mythology, water in lakes, rivers and pools was the home of feminine deities, and also represented the gateway to paradise, which either lay beneath or beyond the water. Here, a pool of water acts as the gateway to the moon, representing intuitive lunar wisdom.

A crab or *crayfish* always appears on this strange card, and is usually thought to symbolize the borders between dreams and the unconscious (water) and physical reality – because this creature can live on the land, too. In Sumerian myth, crabs are the companions of the goddess of the waters.

Land of Dreams

The strange and surreal image of the Moon stands between the naked goddess of the Star and the vibrant daylight of the Sun which follows. This card portrays two dogs guarding the gates of death, howling beside a pool in which a crayfish lives. Above these creatures a full moon rides serenely in the night sky, gazing down upon her kingdom. This is the realm of the High Priestess. Her twin pillars are revealed as turrets, standing on the borders of her unearthly domain. Like the gates of dreams imagined by the Greeks, these towers mark the boundaries between the rational intellect and the rich fertility of the sleeping mind.

Dogs have always belonged to the threshold between life and death, day and night. In Egypt, jackal-headed Anubis presided over the passage of the soul; in Greece, triple-headed Cerberus stood at the gates of Hades. Virgin moon goddesses such as Artemis and Diana hunted with packs of hounds, while the underworld goddess Hecate was also accompanied by dogs. In medieval superstition, dogs could see the Angel of Death; they were often depicted on tombs as faithful companions, resting at the feet of their master or mistress. Dogs are, by nature, sensitive to the moon, often becoming restless or excited when it is full. Since a multiplicity of cultures believed the moon to be the soul's destination after death, this may be the origin of the ancient belief. Dogs and jackals also scavenge for food, feeding on dead flesh as well as hunting for fresh food. Whatever the roots of these beliefs, they are widespread and enduring. A canine howl remains an uncanny and chilling sound that evokes our most primitive fears.

The crayfish or crab on this card has inspired many interpretations. It is primitive life, yet to evolve into warm-blooded forms. It is the sign of Cancer the Crab, a sign ruled by the moon. Ancient astrology held that when all the planets converged in Cancer the world would end. However, the world presented by the tarot trumps does not end, for the darkness of the Moon is followed by the light of the Sun – just as initiates in mystery religions emerged from darkness into daylight to symbolize enlightenment.

The High Priestess has revealed herself to the Fool, who will leave her shadowy kingdom with the wisdom of intuition – a quality associated with Pisces, the zodiac sign which rules this card. Pisces is also the last of the twelve signs, symbolizing the accumulated knowledge and experience of the previous eleven. The three trump cards which follow the Moon have been assigned planets, to symbolize the transcendent nature of the end of the tarot cycle.

Upright Meaning

Since people have always responded to the moon with a mixture of worship and superstition, it is unsurprising that this card evokes similar reactions. However, this is primarily the card of the unconscious mind, so it is linked with all illusory and hidden things.

When describing yourself, or your state of mind, the Moon indicates a flourishing inner life. Intense dreams, compelling visions, intuitive guidance and creative activity can all surface at this time. Fantasy films, fairytales, poetry, music and inspirational writing may all become attractive to you. Any mild depression accompanying this period suggests some resistance to this challenging process.

If it refers to a relationship, the Moon sometimes warns of illusion and delusion with a partner who may not be quite what they seem. A mutual infatuation, feelings of spiritual love and a strong sense of connection may feel very real, but tread warily for you may be under a temporary spell.

The Moon signifies any work that creates illusion or deals with fantasy and dreams. This includes restaurants and clubs that seek to cocoon guests in an intimate atmosphere; the film industry – in particular, films relating to fantasy, science fiction, romance and the surreal; writing fiction and poetry; dream work – including analysis; psychic work or development; visualization techniques; and work connected with water – especially if it has a healing focus.

The Moon often refers to women's health, for it is associated with menstruation and menstrual problems. Because of its connection to dreams, it can denote a deep need for more sleep – a need to enter the dream world and be refreshed by it.

Reversed Meaning

Confusion is signified by the Moon reversed. You may be telling lies, or someone is lying to you. Offers could dissolve, deals fall through, illusions may be shattered. A relationship indicated by this card is plagued with fantasy, and is likely to prove temporary because it is not based on anything real. Drug abuse, alcoholism, depression and withdrawal from the everyday world may cause problems for you, or for someone in your life. Visiting someone in hospital, a convalescent home or even prison is also a possibility. The position of the Moon, its accompanying cards and context will all help you to decide how to interpret this card. The keynote is hidden difficulties – it is not a good time to make any binding commitments.

XIX
THE SUN

RULING PLANET
Sun

KEYWORDS
UPRIGHT: Vitality • Success • Joy
REVERSED: Arrogance • Failure • Delayed joys

SUNFLOWERS were said to symbolize worship and were associated with Apollo and Mithra

LILIES represent fertility, immortality and faith

TWO CHERUBS are based on the heraldic tradition of cherubs as winged children, and represent innocence and joy

SUN is linked with gold, which the alchemists sought to create from base metals – an allegory of spiritual and material wealth

LION is a symbol of masculine power, fortitude, strength and the fiery principle

GREEN BACKGROUND is the colour of life triumphant – an essential meaning of this card

Symbolism of the Card

A GOLDEN LION'S FACE GAZES SERENELY OUT OF THE HEART OF A GLORIOUS NOONDAY SUN. BOTH THE SUN AND THE LION ARE ASSOCIATED WITH THE ROYAL ZODIAC SIGN OF LEO.

The *sun* symbolized the eye of heaven and divinity in a multitude of cultures. Renaissance astronomer Copernicus wrote: 'At the centre of all things resides the sun ... Rightly it is called the lamp, the spirit, the ruler of the universe.'

The sun's symbolic creative power is linked with gold, the most precious of metals; alchemists sought to transform base metals into gold – a profound allegory of spiritual and material wealth.

As an archetypal solar beast, the *lion* is an emblem of masculine power, fortitude, strength and the fiery principle. Sometimes a lion guards the cabbalistic Tree of Life or other treasures. The red alchemical lion denotes the male principle, while the green lion signifies the beginning of the great and hazardous process of transmuting raw materials into the elixir of life, or spiritual enlightenment.

Sunflowers bloom at the top of this card. Resembling the sun itself, they signify the solar principle because they always turn their faces towards the sunlight. For this reason they were said to symbolize worship, and were therefore associated with Apollo, the Greek sun god, and with Persian Mithra.

Lilies climb up each side of this dramatic solar image. These star-like flowers symbolize the feminine principle, representing fertility and immortality. Dante, the early Renaissance poet, named this flower 'the lily of faith' – an important attribute of this card. Lilies were long associated with myriad goddesses, with the archangel Gabriel and with the Virgin Mary.

Two cherubs are dancing in the Sun's garden. These cherubs are based on the heraldic tradition of cherubs as winged children. As such they represent innocence and joy. Physical, intellectual and spiritual children are also linked with the sun in astrology, because the sun's house is the centre of creativity in both zodiac and tarot symbolism.

As a blending of blue and yellow, the vivid, vernal **green background** symbolizes the marriage of intellect (blue) with the heat of emotion (golden yellow). It is the colour of Venus and Mercury, representing a pair of ideal lovers – Venus symbolic of love, Mercury of the rational mind. Above all, this is the colour of life triumphant – an essential meaning of the Sun.

The Eye of the Day

As the visible source of life on earth, the sun has been viewed with awe and reverence for millennia. It was sometimes a male deity, bright and kingly, sometimes a feminine creatrix, always a great power whose movements and eclipses were eagerly observed, and whose loss was deeply feared.

In European myth, the sun was principally associated with Greek Apollo and Persian Mithra. The religion of Mithra, whose official birthday was 25 December, contained many similarities to Christianity. Mithra had twelve apostles, for example, who represented the signs of the zodiac. His miraculous birth, in a cave, was witnessed by shepherds, and the infant deity was visited by sun-priests – or wise men – at his birthplace. Priests of Mithra were celibate. Many features of this earlier religion were assimilated into Christianity because Mithra was a dying and rising saviour who promised heavenly rewards and redemption to his followers. But the motif of dying and experiencing rebirth is a very ancient one, and there are many rituals and ceremonies associated with the sun's apparent death at the northern hemisphere's winter solstice, just before 25 December. Similarly, the rising sun at the spring equinox has been celebrated since prehistory. Many mystery cults adopted the pattern of darkness followed by light triumphant as part of their initiation ceremonies, which were invariably conducted in darkness, often inside caves, tunnels or in underground chambers.

The position of the Sun in the tarot trumps suggests the Fool's emergence from the underworld. The two children on this card symbolize new life, innocence, playfulness and joy – qualities associated with this solar symbol in myth and astrology. In *The Renaissance Tarot* the Sun has a lion's face. The lion is one of the archetypal solar animals, symbolizing sun-ruled Leo, and associated with both the sun and moon in many mythologies. Its dual nature is appropriate to this card which, although generally interpreted as fortunate, can also suggest the fierce, burning heat of the midday sun that can destroy life – just as a hunting lion does. Lions are also symbolic of victory over death – the Fool's voyage through the underworld represents a kind of psychological death, a surrender of old values and beliefs so that something new can be born. In Egypt, the lion symbolized maternity and vengeance, life and death – while the green lion of alchemy represents the elixir and the beginning of the alchemical process. The Fool has found the elixir of wisdom, and now approaches the end of the trumps – and the beginning of a whole new cycle.

THE SUN

Upright Meaning

Joy and vitality flow into any spread where the Sun appears. The happy, positive vibrations of this card are as powerful as the summer sun, lighting up the most sombre reading and minimizing any difficulties indicated by other cards.

Warmth and energy are signified in your work, relationships or social life. An enhanced sense of enjoyment, of pleasure in the details of your life, is always suggested. The Sun often appears in a spread as the golden herald of good times, success, triumph and celebration after a period of effort or withdrawal from the world. These delights may manifest in a number of ways. Worldly success and praise are often suggested. You may bring your dreams to fruition now, or be full of brand-new plans. Your instincts are clear and you are in tune with yourself.

When accompanied by travelling cards, such as the Six of Swords or even the Fool, the Sun suggests an important trip or business links with a hot country. It may indicate the summer season, too, suggesting that this will be an important time of year for success and happiness.

The Sun also represents children. In its most literal interpretation, this card denotes good news concerning children – and may even suggest the birth of a special baby, especially if the Empress appears close by. As with the Empress, the Sun can also refer to a 'brainchild'. If you are enquiring about the success of a project or idea, then the Sun promises abundant rewards and victory – a golden future.

Reversed Meaning

When reversed, the Sun signifies disappointment or failure. This means that arrogance and vanity have caused you to overlook the finer details, or not to put in sufficient hard work to ensure a project's success. This may affect you, or someone you are closely involved with, in business or love. There is an inability to focus on the present moment, leading to careless moves in creativity, love or business.

When signifying children, the Sun indicates difficulties caused by oversensitivity, school problems, allergies or hyperactivity. These problems are not insurmountable, for the Sun remains a positive card even when it is reversed. A new approach is called for, however – resistance to new ideas is often at the root of these difficulties.

Finally, when the rest of your spread is optimistic and fortunate, the Sun reversed simply means delayed success and happiness. When the right time comes, the Sun will shine on you and your efforts.

THE MAJOR ARCANA

— XX —
JUDGEMENT

RULING PLANET
Pluto

KEYWORDS
UPRIGHT: Rebirth • New directions
REVERSED: Delayed decisions • Fear of change

MICHAEL
the archangel is a messenger between the Divine source of creation and human beings

HORN
blown by Michael is a timeless symbol, calling the souls of the dead from their resting places

WINGED HEARTS
symbolize the souls responding to Michael's call and ascending towards new life and rebirth

FLAG
hanging from Michael's horn bears the symbol of Pluto, the planet of rebirth and transformation

Symbolism of the Card

JUDGEMENT DEPICTS THE AWESOME ARCHANGEL, MICHAEL, BLOWING HIS HORN TO CALL THE SOULS OF THE DEAD FROM THEIR RESTING PLACES.

Awakening the soul on the Day of Judgement, and its entry into heaven or descent into hell, was always known as the Last Trump, meaning 'the last call'. This timeless symbol is found all over the world in myths of the last days of the world, and of judgement for one's actions throughout life.

Michael was a warrior angel, fierce and uncompromising. His appearance on such a momentous occasion added to its fabled solemnity and power. All angels are messengers between the Divine source of creation and human beings, and they represent the great unseen powers of the spiritual world. These are the powers the Fool has discovered through the tests and experiences of the tarot journey. Now they are asking to be acknowledged and assimilated, before the cycle begins again with the turning point of the World, the final card in the series of the tarot trumps.

A *flag* hangs from Michael's *horn*, decorated with the symbol of the planet Pluto. Pluto was only discovered in the 1930s, but in astrology it has come to represent the forces of transformation. Even though Renaissance astrologers were unaware of this planet, they were certainly aware of the forces of destiny it has come to symbolize. The motif of death and rebirth is particularly appropriate for both card and planet, and is representative of the journey into the abyss, the discoveries made there, and the re-emergence into the ordinary world, transformed by experience.

Four *winged hearts* fly up towards the angelic figure. These symbolize the souls responding to the angel's call, ascending towards new life and rebirth.

Spirit of Redemption

The card of Judgement depicts the biblical Last Trump, the trumpet call of the archangel Michael summoning the souls of the dead from their resting places. Since the World, the actual last trump card of the sequence, follows this card, Judgement may have been intended as confirmation of the World's deeper meaning as the second turning point of the cards. Judgement, then, is the last trump card, depicting the Last Trump – a typical visual pun from an era which delighted in such things.

The archangel Michael took on

many of the attributes of the god Hermes/Mercury, as conductor of the souls of the dead. Hills and temples sacred to Hermes, messenger god and god of the four quarters of the compass, were often converted into places associated with the archangel Michael. As legendary philosopher, Hermes Trismegistus was said to be the author of many alchemical and philosophical works. Hermetic magic, astrology, alchemy and symbolism were preserved by Arab scholars during the Dark Ages, resurfacing in Europe during the Renaissance. Collections of this lore were named the Corpus Hermeticum – one was presented to the influential Italian Medici family during the mid-fourteenth century. During the Renaissance, Hermetic lore and symbolism fascinated scholars, and its emblems and philosophy were taken very seriously.

Hermes Trismegistus was believed to be a living contemporary of Moses or a grandson of Abraham. This mythic consort of Aphrodite had come a long way and undergone many transformations – a role somehow fitting for the Greek and Roman god of magic.

Judgement is numbered twenty, which in numerology reduces to two – a number of duality, of life and death, body and soul, active and passive. Twenty is also a special number, being the number of fingers and toes on the average human being. The duality symbolized by this card is between the underworld journey in darkness and the arrival of the Fool at the end of his journey to find, in the World which follows, yet another beginning.

Pluto is the planet assigned to this card. Discovered in the 1930s, this planet was named for the god of the dead, and symbolically presides over transformation. As the planet of buried treasure, Pluto represents the treasures of the unconscious mind – creativity and intuition – which the Fool has discovered and borne back from the underworld. The overall message of Judgement is one of renewal. Taken as a Judeo-Christian symbol, it means life everlasting; when related to Hermes/Mercury, it means an ability to return from the underworld; and when interpreted in the context of contemporary astrology it signifies transformation.

Upright Meaning

Essentially, Judgement signifies awakening to a new life, a new self, a fresh flowering of energy and hope. If you have been struggling to make your life work, you will now feel a strong and uplifting sense of renewal. This often springs from an acceptance of the past and all its events. Once free from them, you are effectively reborn and able to enjoy the present moment to the full. Judgement can mean healing on many different levels. It is a card of successful convalescence after illness, of recovery from accidents and from emotional traumas. The untrodden path beckons you, a new life is waiting to be lived.

Judgement can also denote a decision point in your life, where your own judgement should be considered, calm and intuitive. Often, this decision relates to your career, self-expression and way of life. You need to make changes, but these are serious and far-reaching and must not be hurried. A happy outcome is suggested by this deeply serious, but very positive, card. If you are consulting the cards for another person, he or she may need reassurance because they are about to take a big step in life. What lies ahead of them will be described in more detail by other cards in the spread. But, whatever it may be, it is certain to be stimulating, and to be a natural development in life.

Reversed Meaning

Judgement reversed denotes a stagnant phase, brought about by delay in making an important decision. Ambivalence, procrastination or a paralysing fear of change has halted progress and created a claustrophobic atmosphere of tension and doubt. The type of delay signified by reversed Judgement is unhelpful, and will lead to a loss of some kind if action is not taken soon. This may be loss of opportunity or loss of a relationship – and will be clarified by the surrounding cards.

Sometimes reversed Judgement symbolizes a parting within an established relationship or business partnership. This is a temporary pause rather than a permanent split, and may be necessary for such practical reasons as work in another country or city, or for emotional ones, such as a need to reassess a relationship. Final partings are rarely signified because, whether upright or reversed, Judgement is the card of rebirth and the renewal of hope.

THE MAJOR ARCANA

—XXI—
THE WORLD

RULING PLANET
Saturn

KEYWORDS
UPRIGHT: Completion • Fulfilment
REVERSED: Resisting completion

ANGEL
of Aquarius symbolizes the element of air

FEMALE FIGURE
is eternally engaged in a dance of life, death and rebirth and represents the goddesses of wisdom in all cultures

BULL
of Taurus signifies the element of earth

PHOENIX/EAGLE
of Scorpio represents the element of water

OVAL FRAME
signifies the Cosmic Egg of wholeness and wisdom

LION
of Leo symbolizes the element of fire

Symbolism of the Card

THE WORLD OR MAJOR FORTUNE REPRESENTS THE COMPLETION OF THE TAROT TRUMPS, AND THE DAWNING OF THE NEXT CYCLE.

The World is paired with the Wheel of Fortune, which reflects the same message in a lesser fashion. The *female figure* on this card is eternally engaged in the dance of life, death and rebirth. If the tarot represents a spiritual journey, then the World signifies both its end and its beginning. This female figure symbolizes the goddesses of wisdom in all cultures who presided over life and death. Glimpses of the goddesses are found all the way through the tarot trumps, and here they are amalgamated into one shining deity, mother of all gods and goddesses since the dawn of time. Her nakedness symbolizes this revelation and confirms the pagan heritage of the cards and their dreamlike symbols.

The goddess dances within an *oval frame*, symbolic of the Cosmic Egg of wholeness and wisdom. The Cosmic Egg and the Ouroboros or circular serpent are really one and the same symbol, along with the wreath that is so often depicted on the World. All these symbols, which are related to the wheel, the circle and the symbol for feminine gender, represent the cycles of destiny that are constantly manifesting in our lives. These circular symbols also represent the womb of the mother goddess, the cosmic gateway of life and the gateway through which we must all pass at the point of death.

Symbolic creatures representing the four elements, the four fixed signs of the zodiac and the four compass points are placed in the four corners. This echoes the design for the Wheel of Fortune, linking the two cards together as Major and Minor Fortune. On the World they symbolize wholeness and completion, because the various experiences they represent have been absorbed and understood.

Mystical Mandala

A woman dances inside a wreath of leaves or flowers on traditional images of the last trump card. As a mandala image, it symbolizes the first and last turning point of the tarot sequence and is paired with the Wheel of Fortune for this reason. In some old tarot decks the World is called the Major Fortune, to emphasize the link between these two cards.

As a symbol, it is usually said to represent the great goddess who created the world in so many ancient mythologies. The oval ellipse that usually frames the female figure is a widespread symbol of feminine gender. It was often used in the Middle Ages as a surround for paintings of the Virgin Mary, symbolizing her ascent into heaven. This shape is known as a mandorla, almond or vesica piscis and is associated with goddess worship in oriental art. The two sides of this mystical almond represent a gateway, the womb of the goddess, just as the World is a gateway to the next cycle. As a flame symbol, the mandorla means soul and spirit.

For the Gnostics, alchemists and those who studied esoteric Judaism (cabbala), the World represented Sophia, spirit of wisdom and bride of God. She has many guises and is also known as Philosophia, Sapienta, the Shekina, or female spirit of God. There is a beautiful woodcut portrait of Philosophia by Albrecht Dürer (1502) showing her inside a wreath of fruits and flowers. In each corner are symbols of the four seasons, elements and ages of mankind. This picture, which bears a strong similarity to the World, illustrates the work of Dürer's friend Conrad Celtis (1459–1508). Part of the inscription reads: 'That which constitutes the essence of heaven, earth, air and water, and that which embraces the life of man, as well as that which the fiery God creates in the whole world: I, Philosophia, bear all in my breast.'

As Sophia, she represented the Gnostic Mother Goddess, whose smile caused the soul of the World to be born. Sophia even found her way into the Bible, where she makes a speech in which she says, 'I am understanding; I have strength.' These are the enduring treasures that the Fool has discovered and brought back from the underworld.

The World has been allocated Saturn as its planetary ruler. Saturn was the last planet known to ancient astrologers, who called it Rex Mundi or King of the World. As stern gatekeeper, Saturn ruled time and the many cycles of life – just as the World symbolizes progression and rebirth, for it stands at the conclusion of the tarot story and presides over the birth of the beginning of the next phase.

Upright Meaning

The World signifies completion, fulfilment and achievement. The end of a long cycle now draws to a close in your life. This often represents a major accomplishment, such as a creative project, fulfilment of a dream or successful conclusion to a course of education. It is time to say farewell, and to celebrate this pinnacle in your life. Some kind of ritual often accompanies this card, whether it is the opening of your first exhibition, a degree ceremony, a significant promotion at work, an engagement or marriage. Important moments in life are signified here – life is about to change its rhythm as it enters a brand-new phase. Starting a family is sometimes signified, especially if accompanied by the Empress or Ten of Cups. Retirement is another life experience symbolized by the World, especially when it means freedom to pursue other interests or develop in new directions.

When describing a relationship, the World promises happiness and the renewal of understanding between you. Again, a new cycle opens up and may bring a change of home, country or circumstances for you both. The other cards will clarify this, and reveal the precise shape these changes may take.

The World can denote journeys, just as the Fool may sometimes herald travelling. In this instance, the card relates to adventures which expand your inner world as well as offering new experiences, sights and sounds. Ultimately, the World is a fortunate, joyful and immensely satisfying influence on any spread in which it appears. It signifies the right time for you to taste joy and success, before the next stage of your journey begins to unfold.

Reversed Meaning

The World signifies inevitable change and development. When it is reversed there is some delay before the pattern can be completed. Unfinished emotional business may be affecting your relationship, or the inability to complete a project or perhaps even to begin it. Some kind of test faces you, and you are uncertain and hesitant about doing what needs to be done. Cutting the ties that bind you to the past is the most positive thing that you can do now. For it is the past that is blocking your progress and preventing natural and positive changes from taking place in your life. Forget your fears and let go. The changes signified by the World are always happy, productive ones.

Part Two

THE MINOR ARCANA

THE MINOR ARCANA, OR LESSER SECRETS, IS A DECK OF FIFTY-SIX CARDS. IT IS VERY SIMILAR TO THE FAMILIAR 'PLAYING' CARDS OF TODAY, WITH ITS NUMBERED PIP CARDS AND COURT CARDS. THE PIP CARDS MAY PREDATE AND CERTAINLY CORRESPOND TO THE FOUR SUITS OF PLAYING CARDS: WANDS, STAVES OR BATONS ARE CLUBS; PENTACLES, DISCS OR COINS ARE DIAMONDS; SWORDS ARE SPADES; AND CUPS OR VESSELS ARE HEARTS.

Mythic Origins

The mythic origins of all these symbols can be traced to sacred Hindu art, in which the cup, ring, sceptre and sword are emblems of life's stages and themes. The four magical treasures of Celtic mythology were the cauldron, spear, stone and sword. And Nemesis, the formidable, all-seeing Greek goddess of fate, possessed a cup, wand, wheel and sword. The four suits also represent the idea of balance between masculine and feminine forces, a notion that is fundamental to oriental medicine and geomancy (Feng Shui). Swords and Wands symbolize the phallic, masculine energies of air and fire, which are imagined as active and penetrating. Cups and Pentacles are symbolically female, the receptive and nurturing elements of water and earth respectively.

The court cards, too, present a natural balance between male and female energies. The King and Queen complement one another, while the Knight and Page symbolize male and female qualities in nascent form. In some decks the Page is depicted as a Princess. For *The Renaissance Tarot* we have chosen an androgynous Page, a figure that can represent either sex or alternatively can symbolize an alchemical blending of their qualities. Inner androgyny was one of the most powerful symbolic aims of alchemy, and also of oriental Tantric philosophy.

The Lesser Secrets are vital for any balanced reading, contributing invaluable detail and finer shades of meaning to the whole picture. Indeed, the very words 'minor' and 'lesser' are rather misleading, for these cards possess great subtlety and fluidity of their own. The Lesser Secrets reveal details, often describe passing states of mind and highlight the precise focus of a tarot spread. While the vibrant, archetypal images of the Major Arcana present overall themes, the Minor cards sketch in the background against which these themes are acted out. So the Lovers might denote an all-encompassing love affair when accompanied by appropriate cards from the suit of Cups. But if surrounded by Wands and Pentacles, the Lovers' other meaning – choice – would then relate to the work and money issues that are symbolized by these suits.

The four suits of the Minor Arcana are linked with the zodiac signs, with the four elements of the ancient world, with the four basic psychological types and a number of other correspondences. Such associations were fundamental to the mystical world-view – the idea that everything is connected with everything else. In this philosophy, whose roots lie at the heart of astrology, geomancy, divination, magic and alchemy, the Cosmos is pictured as one vast, living entity. Every part contributes to the greater whole, and thus has meaning and value. The ancient hermetic dictum, 'As above, so below', sums up the idea that everything on earth mirrors the awesome workings of the Universal Mind.

Correspondences and the Minor Arcana				
	Wands	**Pentacles**	**Swords**	**Cups**
Element	Fire	Earth	Air	Water
Elemental Spirit	Salamander	Earth Spirit	Sylph	Merfolk/Undine
Season	Summer	Winter	Spring	Autumn
Time	Midday	Midnight	Sunrise	Sunset
Psychological Function	Intuition	Senses/Instinct	Thinking	Feeling
Zodiac Signs	Aries, Leo, Sagittarius	Taurus, Virgo, Capricorn	Gemini, Libra, Aquarius	Cancer, Scorpio, Pisces
Keyword	Energy	Structure	Logic	Receptivity
Highest Power	Vision	Wisdom	Clarity	Love

THE MINOR ARCANA

The Four Elements and the Minor Arcana

In *The Renaissance Tarot* the four elements are each given their own mythical spirit beings, timeless creatures of the imagination which people fairytales and myths around the world. These creatures of the Minor Arcana relate to Renaissance symbolism, magic, medicine and philosophy. They are embodiments of the four elements of fire, earth, air and water – the principles believed at the time to be the building blocks of the entire world and every living thing within it. Each elemental kingdom has its own ambience, its characteristic inhabitants, colours and sphere of influence.

The first suit, Wands, belongs to the element of fire. Its creatures are jinnees, fire beings whose Arabic name has been Anglicized to 'genie'. The word 'genius' stems from 'genie' and meant 'spirit' in medieval times. These ideas are all linked to the idea of inspiration, which is embodied by the suit of Wands.

The second suit, Pentacles, represents the element of earth. Earth spirits have been given many names in different cultures – gnomes, elves, brownies, dwarfs, trolls, satyrs, centaurs and so on. We have chosen to depict creatures made of leaves, which are closely linked to the Green Man of pagan Europe, the dryads or tree spirits of classical myth, and ultimately Dionysus, anarchic Indo-European god of the vine. All these beings are associated with the senses, with the tangible world – whether through buried treasure, healing, mining the earth's mineral wealth or through exuberant revelry. So, they resonate with the overall theme of the Pentacles, which is one of practical sensuality.

The third suit, Swords, rules the invisible element of air, as well as the unseen world of thought and mental activity. In the kingdom of air, the traditional inhabitants are sylphs, angels and all other winged beings. In alchemy, quicksilver or mercury is symbolized by wings to show its volatile and changeable nature. Aerial spirits communicated with human beings through the winds and breezes. In their highest expression they denote free spirits, transcending the mundane world of matter. At their most baleful, they resemble the devastating effects of a hurricane, or the unsettling influence of winds such as the French mistral. Similarly, in Shakespeare's words, 'There is nothing good or bad but thinking makes it so.' The mind and its thoughts may be turned to positive or negative account.

Finally, the suit of Cups belongs to the element of water. Water beings are in many mythologies from ancient Babylon to Polynesia. Archetypal water spirits are most often personified in Western art and iconography as mermaids and mermen – the creatures we have chosen for *The Renaissance Tarot*. Travellers' tales, sailors' yarns and poignant fairytales all celebrate these mysterious water divinities, who are often linked, like the suit of Cups itself, with conscious sacrifice, passion, love and seduction.

Numerology and the Minor Arcana

The four suits of the Minor Arcana comprise ten pip cards, plus the King, Queen, Knight and Page. Each suit represents one of the four elements – fire, earth, air and water – believed for many centuries to form the foundations of every living thing. Clearly, each suit is a family, with its own symbolic energies. These correspond to numbers one to ten of the Major Arcana, representing the first cycle of initiation and life experience that these cards depict. However, it is helpful to know that each group of cards that bear the same numerical value are also linked together. So, each Ace, for example, represents inception – the birth of an energy that is particular to its own suit. By understanding the collective ruling number of each group you can quickly begin to grasp the underlying structure of the Minor Arcana. By combining this number with its element you will soon learn the basic meaning of every card, and be able to fill in the finer details as you progress. The following table shows you the core meanings of each group:

Card	Principle	Major Arcana	Keywords
Aces	Consciousness	Magician	Inception, energy
Twos	Synthesis	High Priestess	Blending, balancing
Threes	Growth	Empress	Fertility, creativity
Fours	Form	Emperor	Endurance, stability
Fives	Conflict	Hierophant	Change, struggle, spirit
Sixes	Harmony	Lovers	Fortune through effort
Sevens	Mutability	Chariot	Temporary situations
Eights	Power	Justice/Strength	Gain and sacrifice
Nines	Completion	Hermit	Purification and progress
Tens	Transformation	Wheel of Fortune	Karma and consolidation

THE SUIT OF WANDS

As the first suit of the Minor Arcana, the suit of Wands begins the sequence of fifty-six cards with a burst of fiery, visionary energy. Wands are linked to the fire signs of the zodiac – Aries, Leo and Sagittarius. Symbolic of optimistic action on the inner and outer planes of reality, Wands emphasize the power of intuitive inspiration. All creative thinkers draw on this dramatic, volatile force. It may manifest as an inspired artistic triumph, a ground-breaking political manoeuvre or a brilliant business coup but, whatever form events symbolized by Wands may take, the characteristic boldness of fire will be their signature.

Resonance and Dissonance – What to Look for

All suits of the Minor Arcana are weakened or strengthened by their companions. This is called resonance and dissonance, and is based upon the elemental and symbolic meanings of each suit of the Minor Arcana. Some combine well and bring out the best in each other, others have little in common and reduce one another's effectiveness. The active, positive vibrations of Wands are objective; that is, they tend to describe events that have an impact on the visible world. Wands are enhanced by the presence of Swords and Pentacles, but are undermined by the presence of Cups. The energies of Wands are channelled into the world of ideas with Swords, and into the world of practical achievement when combined with Pentacles. When paired with a number of Cups, however, their fires are dampened, emotions become unstable and creative expression lacks focus.

Traditional Areas of Influence

Each Wand has a specific meaning. Yet each suit, as a whole, governs a particular sphere. When Wands predominate in a spread it will tend to focus on the following:

• Travel, whether mental, physical or spiritual – this embraces exploring all terrains: intellectual adventures, holidays and travelling, spiritual inner voyages and leaps of imagination.

• All deals, negotiations and speculations are ruled by Wands, which have a particular affinity with property, publishing, entertainment and innovative enterprises.

• Career, as defined by dreams, visions, wishes and life direction, is also governed by Wands. This is defined in terms of broad concepts such as service to others, self-expression, risk-taking, inventiveness and so on. Such concepts identify the compelling theme of someone's life pattern rather than spell out the details of daily routine.

ACE OF WANDS

KEYWORDS
UPRIGHT: Inception • Vision • Energy
REVERSED: Fire • Ice

Symbolism of the Card

The Ace of Wands stands amidst the flames of its ruling element, supported in heraldic fashion by a pair of salamanders. Salamanders often symbolized the element of fire. These fierce creatures represent enduring courage which cannot be destroyed by difficulty. Glyphs for the three fire signs, Aries, Leo and Sagittarius, are shown above the Ace of Wands.

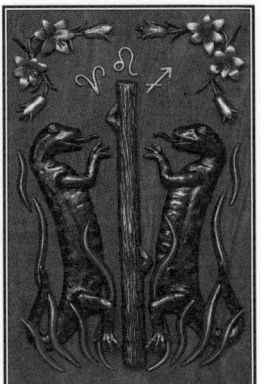

Upright Meaning

Each Ace denotes a beginning, the nature of which is particular to its ruling element. Here, the positive, vibrant energies of fire convey the idea of creative power, the birth of innovative and imaginative projects.

Most often, this card signifies revitalizing energies that transform the working and creative life. So, you are looking for fresh ideas, new directions, all that is inventive, original and exciting. The Ace of Wands also stimulates an interest in self-development – you may want to learn new skills or enhance established ones. Any new projects or endeavours are favoured, as is any activity needing renewed energy or optimism.

The symbolic meaning of conception, gestation and birth usually relates to ideas and projects when the Ace of Wands appears. But this card can indicate physical fertility when the surrounding cards concur. It can also represent the completion of a product, successful deal, contract or work of creative imagination, such as a painting, play, book or piece of music.

Reversed Meaning

When the Ace of Wands is reversed, the flames of creative energy are quenched. Creative blocks, disappointing delays and frustrated plans are all suggested.

In love, there may be emotional repression, physical frigidity, impotence or sterility. For reasons described by the surrounding cards, the creative and emotional arena is temporarily barren. The desire to change this state of affairs may be frustrated in the immediate future, but new directions or ways of approaching the problem should appear to help you soon.

TWO OF WANDS

KEYWORDS
UPRIGHT: **Balance of power**
REVERSED: **Disharmony**

Symbolism of the Card

This card combines the creative power of fire with the idea of balance that is symbolized by all the Twos in the Minor Arcana. A figure with outstretched arms holds two wands aloft in a triumphant gesture, like a dancer or musician. When power and energy are balanced between active and receptive, true victory is possible.

Upright Meaning

The Two of Wands is connected with prosperous partnerships, productive working relationships and successful speculations. It can also indicate an influential business person who offers inspiration or opportunity.

Traditionally, this card promises success in all deals where negotiation is important. Ideally, each group is satisfied, each person 'wins'. Typically, the Two of Wands symbolizes property deals or the marketing of goods and services. Any deals denoted by this card are operating under fortunate influences and, if other cards agree, you will profit from your efforts.

The balance of power that this card represents manifests as ambition and drive, balanced by inner discipline, restraint and a desire for harmony. In this way, visible success and material achievement are balanced by an awareness of the transient nature of all things.

Reversed Meaning

Difficulties in partnerships, such as disharmony, are symbolized by the Two of Wands reversed. In the working life, this means that a particular association could be coming to an end, for it no longer contributes to the well-being of those involved. It can also mean problems caused by obstinate, greedy or arrogant people – generally connected to work or financial matters.

When denoting current deals or projects, the reversed Two of Wands warns of delays, disruptions and unforeseen expenses. You may not be able to proceed easily – it would be better to wait, or to abandon the project and look for something simpler. Now is not the time to fight for your ideas, ambitions or desires. It is time to reassess your plans and come up with a brand-new strategy.

THE SUIT OF WANDS

THREE OF WANDS

KEYWORDS
UPRIGHT: Opportunity • Expansion • Success
REVERSED: Failure

Symbolism of the Card

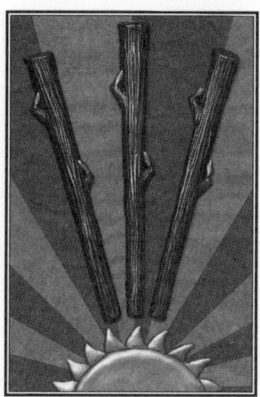

The Three of Wands connects the active, productive qualities of the number three with the creative energies of fire. This is symbolized by the three wands set against a background of the rising sun. Ideas and projects begun under the influence of the Ace (inception) and Two (balance) now flourish in the light of a new dawn.

may represent helpful advice, practical or financial aid, or valuable opportunities in your career. Anything, in fact, which enables you to expand, to develop, or to succeed in your chosen field. It is important to remember that these positive events are invariably linked with past efforts and initiatives. The number three concerns growth, which cannot take place without preparation.

Upright Meaning

Successful progress is symbolized by the Three of Wands. It has strong links with the past – whatever you have been working towards will now begin to show results. Past experience, personal contacts and completed projects may all give rise to opportunities at this time. It is now possible to build on the foundations you have already laid. This card traditionally favours trade and commerce, communicators and writers, inventors and entrepreneurs. It heralds increased profits, many valid ideas and an ability to make long-held dreams come true.

When it is supported by appropriate cards, the Three of Wands

Reversed Meaning

Loss and failure are denoted by the Three of Wands reversed. Failure to grasp opportunities through pride, arrogance or an inability to compromise is a common manifestation of this card. When appropriate, it can symbolize the failure of a dream or beloved project. This is generally due to poor communication of ideas, badly presented concepts, or projects whose time has not yet arrived. Sometimes a plan was simply overambitious and lacked sufficient practical support. It is not the right time to forge ahead; it is time to be practical, realistic and to overcome disappointment.

FOUR OF WANDS

KEYWORDS

UPRIGHT: Harvest • Self-esteem • Home comforts
REVERSED: Delayed benefits

Symbolism of the Card

This card connects fire's expansive energies with the inherent stability of four, which is the number of foundation. The result is a rich sense of security, of harvest. Four wands are arranged like a traditional stook of corn or wheat, and two ears of grain serve to underline the harvest message of this card.

Upright Meaning

The Four of Wands is a joyful card, signifying well-earned rewards, prosperity and a profound sense of satisfaction. Since Wands often denote property matters, this card frequently relates to a new home or improvements to an existing property. 'Home' can indicate refuge, beloved environment, a place with atmosphere and meaning. A second home is sometimes indicated, too.

When describing the working life, the Four of Wands represents the harvesting of success and satisfaction of completing a project or launching a business. This card traditionally represents property matters, music, dance, theatre and entertainment. It is now possible to relax a little and enjoy the results of any sustained past efforts. An inner sense of quiet confidence, self-esteem and harmony is often signified by this card. Four is the number of foundation, suggesting that these positive feelings will form the basis for future development and personal growth.

Reversed Meaning

The positive qualities of the Four of Wands remain even in the reversed position. All the good things promised in its upright position are still possible, although you should expect some delays – especially when enquiring about property deals. Delays require patience, however. Without it, this card suggests anxiety, nervous tension and a restless state of mind. Since success is forecast, it would be more productive to relax and play the waiting game.

The other meaning is a break or gap in the working life. It may be unplanned, such as redundancy, or represent a brief period of unemployment. Since this is an active card, it denotes a busy time after a short delay.

FIVE OF WANDS

KEYWORDS

UPRIGHT: **Competition • Creative conflict**
REVERSED: **Suppressed rage • Battles**

Symbolism of the Card

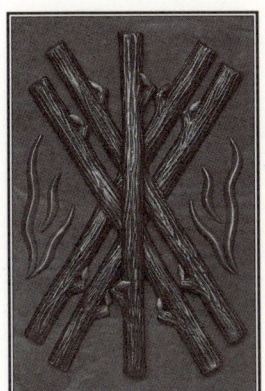

The Five of Wands links the creative qualities of fire with the idea of change and conflict suggested by the number five. Five wands are presented in an interlinked pattern of four, symbolizing conflict, with one central stave standing firm, symbolizing what will emerge from the struggle. Flames flicker on each side, but energy is present too. Situations change and shift rapidly, and the struggle and effort are actually necessary if progress is to be made. Dead wood will be cut out, unworkable ideas rejected and hidden agendas revealed. Whether this manifests as a spiritual or psychological process, a management crisis or clashes between colleagues, it is both a test and a game. What emerges has been refined, clarified and improved.

Upright Meaning

All fives are volatile, and none more so than the Five of Wands. Conflict, competition, arguments and power struggles are all likely to erupt when this card appears. These may manifest at work, when colleagues disagree or a team has difficulties in working together.

Alternatively, an inner conflict is denoted – perhaps conflicting ambitions, uncertainty about career direction or over creative expression. However, although this conflict resembles a battle it is more like a game of skill and subtlety. So it must not be taken too seriously. Creative energies are present, situa-

Reversed Meaning

When reversed, the Five of Wands still carries the message of conflict. Generally, it denotes legal conflicts, litigation and court cases. But, like its upright interpretation, it can also describe inner tension resulting from an inability to act, to make a final commitment or decision. Suppressed anger is often the problem; when not expressed directly it tends to give rise to evasive action, prevarication and other passively hostile acts. Look at the surrounding cards carefully – if they are positive, the outcome of this battle will be entirely positive although a recovery period will be much needed.

SIX OF WANDS

KEYWORDS

UPRIGHT: Victory • Good news
REVERSED: Temporary troubles

Symbolism of the Card

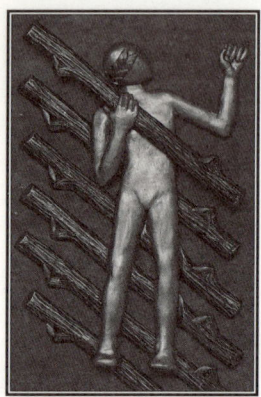

The Six of Wands joins the uplifting energies of fire with the harmonious vibrations of the number six. A wreathed figure raises one hand in victory. The laurel wreath is a multicultural symbol of happiness and glory. The five wands beneath and behind the figure denote past efforts, and the sixth wand is carried over the shoulder, signifying a weapon that is no longer needed.

Upright Meaning

The Six of Wands is a card of joyful celebration, signifying triumph over adversity and victory after hard work and struggle. The wreath worn by the figure on this card is deeply symbolic of the card's inner meaning, for there were several kinds of wreath in the ancient world. As the joyful crown it symbolized a happy fate and was worn by brave soldiers and triumphant athletes. But as the funeral crown it was a symbol of death and mourning. The bridal wreath held two meanings – joy and fertility, and the death of an old life and birth of a new one. Similarly, the Six of Wands denotes good fortune but warns that this is temporary. This is a lucky, happy phase in life but is not permanent.

On a mundane level, the card signifies legal triumphs, beneficial property transactions, promotion and respect at work, successful negotiations and sought-after contracts.

Reversed Meaning

When this card is reversed it indicates conflict and confrontation through others. Typically, this occurs at work, during financial negotiations – perhaps with a bank – and above all through the triumph of another. A promotion or other cherished goal will be given to someone else, causing feelings of betrayal. This sense of betrayal may come in other ways too, by being let down or misled by another person – usually at work, in money matters or when buying and selling products or services. In this instance, the triumph and victory belong to another. But just as the good fortune promised by this card is a stage, so is the failure. As the saying goes, this too will pass.

SEVEN OF WANDS

KEYWORDS
UPRIGHT: **The last battle**
REVERSED: **Loss through fear**

Symbolism of the Card

The Seven of Wands links volatile fire with unstable, changeable seven – a mysterious, mutable number. A figure carries one wand in a defensive manner, to symbolize battles and struggles. Behind the figure, the six crossed wands signify the tense, conflicting vibrations of this card.

if they are to manifest their dreams. Unless this is the final card of a spread, the surrounding cards should confirm eventual success – but only if the challenge is accepted and the fight continues. It would be unwise to give up at this stage, when success is so close at hand.

Upright Meaning

The Seven of Wands, like the Five of Wands, carries a message of conflict and battle. However, where the Five resembles a game, the Seven resembles the battle that decides the final outcome of the struggle. There is more to gain and more to lose. Because seven is a mystical number this struggle is most frequently found as an inner battle, a valiant attempt to maintain the harmony found in the Six of Wands. So, for example, if the Six signified a promotion, the Seven would denote the challenges of new responsibilities.

This card often appears when someone is very tired, and perhaps feels as if all the fight has gone out of them. Yet he or she is required to make one last effort, one final push,

Reversed Meaning

When reversed, the Seven of Wands warns against fear and hesitation. These emotions often appear disguised as a 'provisional' attitude towards life – 'When I can afford it', 'When I have the time', 'When I get married', 'When I get divorced', and so on. The reversed Seven of Wands reminds us that this imaginary time may never come, and that it is fear which is really holding us back. Loss of opportunity, waste of talent, refusal to explore alternatives – all these may be signified here.

This card advises taking action, seeking support and encouragement, and looking for paths out of the dark forest. It is time to take responsibility and to create a more interesting future for yourself.

EIGHT OF WANDS

KEYWORDS
UPRIGHT: Movement • Expansion
REVERSED: Restriction • Frustration

Symbolism of the Card

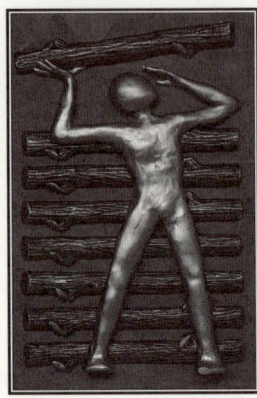

Eight is the number of power and strength. When expressed through Wands, fire's energy is channelled into tangible expansion. A figure looks towards the far horizon, in front of a firm structure of seven wands. The eighth wand is held aloft, a gesture that symbolizes progress and future development.

Upright Meaning

After the inner conflicts of the Seven, the Eight of Wands brings a welcome burst of energy into the progression of this suit. Movement and expansion are signified; this card often indicates a journey, or exciting and important news and communications – the movement of ideas. Life is about to expand – through business success, enhanced social life or even a new romantic interest, especially when paired with the Two or Nine of Cups. The accompanying cards will reveal more details and describe which area of life is about to be especially active.

As the significator of every type of new horizon, the Eight of Wands often heralds travel, important trips and a love of change. There is a longing for freedom, for wild landscapes and for adventure. The Sun or the Chariot may appear, and would confirm this interpretation. The Wheel of Fortune is another Major Arcana card that would underline the feeling of energy and movement in a spread. The sense of power and energy symbolized by this card is like electricity – it will flow where it is directed, but it must be given a channel and an appropriate outlet.

Reversed Meaning

Eight is the number of power but also of restriction because, like four, it represents foundation and structure. When the Eight of Wands is reversed, energy is restricted, resulting in frustration, mistakes and delayed movement of all kinds. Specifically, this tends to manifest in transport difficulties caused by strikes, breakdowns and disputes. In the realm of ideas, it denotes rash decisions resulting in later restriction and advises against signing documents or writing letters of agreement or commitment.

NINE OF WANDS

KEYWORDS
UPRIGHT: Strength • Caution
REVERSED: Depleted energy • Neglect

Symbolism of the Card

The Nine of Wands links the concept of completion, symbolized by the number nine, with fire's volatile energies. An upright figure stretches out, surveying nine wands behind him or her. This represents the element of analysis in this card. The wands are arranged in a sunrise pattern, to denote the dawning of success and the end of a cycle.

Upright Meaning

The Nine of Wands completes the cycle of creative and intuitive progress signified by the suit of Wands. Its presence in a spread affirms achievement, success and recovery from illness or other challenging chains of events. However, because this is a Nine, not a Ten (representing transcendent completion), it suggests a lingering insecurity or uncertainty. It is currently difficult to accept success or to realize the true extent of your own strengths and talents. You have not fully drawn on your abundant reserves of energy and inspiration because you do not realize they are available to you. You could be faced by a challenging situation in the near future; you will need to gather yourself together for one last effort before you achieve your goals.

When partnered by other 'success' cards – perhaps the Ace or Nine of Pentacles – the Nine of Wands advises caution. Embrace success, but do not become careless or overly relaxed. Maintain a sharp eye for detail, stay vigilant over written documents and remain guarded in conversation with others. There could be one final minor obstacle or change to your plans.

Reversed Meaning

Depleted energies are suggested by the Nine of Wands reversed. Often, physical neglect is the root cause – typically, poor diet, prolonged lack of sleep, lack of exercise. Exhaustion results, fire's energies are, quite literally, burned out. At its most benign and positive, the Nine of Wands reversed simply means delayed success. The completion of a project or negotiation process is out of your hands now, but matters will be resolved at a later date.

TEN OF WANDS

KEYWORDS
UPRIGHT: Ambition • Burden of power
REVERSED: Relaxation of responsibility

Symbolism of the Card

The Ten of Wands depicts a figure climbing up steps consisting of nine wands. A single wand, carried like a spear, symbolizes the determination to ascend ever higher up the ladder of success, to keep fighting when others have given up or stood aside. Transcendent number ten combines with fire's love of power to represent both culmination and new beginnings.

Upright Meaning

There is tremendous energy and power in the Ten of Wands. Characteristically, this is directed towards the career, status and visible achievement. Assertive action and ambition combine in what can be an obsessive pursuit of glory and power. Overwork is common, resulting in a self-created burden, driven behaviour, a single-minded quest for applause and public recognition.

Achievement and results are signified but there may be a price to pay. This card warns of imbalance, misuse of power and an overwhelming need to control. When someone is unable to delegate, allow others to play their part or to take independent action, they are afraid to lose control. Ultimately, this need for control becomes a burden which undermines progress. Any Swords in the spread will underline this interpretation. Where cards denoting emotional or physical problems appear, the Ten of Wands stands for a period of overwork that interferes with a balanced life, with pleasure and with faith in the natural progress of things. Reassess your priorities, trust in yourself and relax.

Reversed Meaning

The message of culmination – linked to all Tens – is very clear here. It is time to rest, to celebrate your success and share your happiness with everyone involved. Promotion, recognition, completion of an important project – all are signified. A phase of intense concentration or sustained effort has been completed and must be acknowledged. The ability to share responsibility is significant here; when reversed, this card suggests that there is a much more balanced approach to life.

PAGE~PRINCESS OF WANDS

KEYWORDS
UPRIGHT: Activity • Creative beginnings
REVERSED: Instability • Misdirected energy

Symbolism of the Card

The Page~Princess of Wands is shown as an androgynous young fire spirit, accompanied by sunflower motifs and a fiery lion, both of which have links with the Wands' element of fire. Sunflowers turn their heads to follow the sun, denoting movement of energy; the lion is a solar, fiery creature – here, it is emblematic of the creative energy brought by the Page~Princess of Wands.

Upright Meaning

The Page~Princess of Wands represents the creative, intuitive vibrations of this suit in nascent form. All Pages can be quite subtle in their effects, so if necessary look to the surrounding cards for more clarification. As a herald or messenger card, it indicates an upsurge of internal energy and a quickening of the pace in everyday life. Original ideas, intuitive guidance, a desire to make new friends – all these may spring from inside ourselves. Outer events mirror this energy; there is often an increase in conversations, letters, invitations, short trips and social events. As a significator, the Page of Wands denotes a lively, outgoing child or young teenager of either sex – or one born under a fire sign (Aries, Leo, Sagittarius).

Reversed Meaning

Instability prevails in negotiations, property transactions, short trips, communications, ideas and general progress. As a significator, the Page~Princess of Wands reversed represents a child who may be hyperactive, have literacy problems or be generally disruptive.

Abstract Meaning

When upright and positive, the Page~Princess of Wands has the same meaning as the Page when interpreted as a messenger card. Energy manifests in movement, communications and career areas. When reversed, this card primarily indicates delays, cancelled or postponed journeys and disrupted communications of every kind. Slow progress is generally confirmed by a number of reversed cards in a spread, or sometimes by the nearby presence of the Hanged Man.

KNIGHT OF WANDS

KEYWORDS
UPRIGHT: Impetuous • Sociable
REVERSED: Conflict • Procrastination

Symbolism of the Card

The Knight of Wands is depicted as an ebullient fire spirit, accompanied by a pair of lions. He dances like a freshly lit fire, symbolizing the swift-moving feeling of this card. His lions represent the vigour, enthusiasm and solar principles linked to this card.

Upright Meaning

This card usually represents a young man of intelligence and charm. Extrovert and active, his impetuous nature leads him into many social circles and numerous activities. He generates great enthusiasm but may find sustained action a challenge. Starting projects is simple, completing them is another matter. He is agile, often fit, and loves games and sports. He may also stand for someone born under Aries, Leo or Sagittarius.

Occasionally, the volatile Knight of Wands signifies an older man with boyish qualities. However, his initial charms soon wear thin. He is unable to commit to anything, shies away from responsibility and wants his partner to play the parent to his child in any form of love relationship. As a colleague, he can prove unreliable and often fails to explore his considerable creative potential.

Reversed Meaning

When reversed, the Knight of Wands retains his magnetic charms but this time they are not to be trusted. He lies easily, procrastinates and tends to create trouble and resentment wherever he goes. His limited beliefs and narrow-minded viewpoint often lead to arguments and conflicts. He may be a fanatic, a bully or a pompous bore.

Abstract Meaning

Swift actions, sudden decisions and unexpected trips or changes of home are all signified by the Knight of Wands. He is also linked with politics of every persuasion, from anarchy to military organizations. Similarly, this card can denote religious groups and cults, usually those with strong political leanings or connections. The position of this card, the type of spread being used and the context in which it is read must all be taken into account here.

THE SUIT OF WANDS

QUEEN OF WANDS

KEYWORDS

UPRIGHT: Warmth • Loyalty • Pleasure
REVERSED: Vengeful • Domineering

TRADITIONALLY, THIS CARD REPRESENTS A WOMAN WHO IS CONNECTED WITH TRAVEL AND SPECULATIVE VENTURES.

Symbolism of the Card

The Queen of Wands is a female fire spirit, shown here with sunflowers and a playful dragon. This is a suitable companion because dragons are creatures of fable that are often depicted as breathing fire – the element represented by the suit of Wands. Legends involving the slaying of dragons describe the triumph of the conscious mind over unconscious fears and behaviour patterns.

Upright Meaning

The Queen of Wands personifies the fiery goddesses of old, whose chariots were drawn by lions or who rode lions as symbols of their creative powers. These vibrant figures were maternal, fierce, loving and frequently war-like. They, like the Queen of Wands when she is in her highest manifestation, symbolize the warming, life-giving powers of the sun and of fire. Yet such blazing energies may also destroy life, hence the vengeful attributes of the reversed Queen. Like the glittering Russian Firebird, or seductive Sumerian Ishtar, the Queen of Wands has compelling glamour and dazzling powers of attraction. She is the glowing heart of fire, for good or ill.

As a woman, the Queen of Wands represents a loyal friend, playful lover and enthusiastic colleague. She is protective and supportive of close friends and family, generous, hospitable and inspirational. Her sense of humour and positive attitudes help her to make progress, win friends and survive set-backs with panache and style.

In personal relationships, the Queen of Wands is passionate and sensual. Her fiery intensity is lightened by her vital, fun-loving nature and proud independence. While she is loving and confident, she also needs reassurance and appreciation to flourish; her inner fire must be fed. She dislikes possessive people and cannot bear to feel trapped by her friend, colleague or lover.

She may abruptly withdraw from any relationship where she feels cornered, taken for granted or exhausted by others' demands. As a simple significator, this card denotes women born under the three fire signs of the zodiac – Aries, Leo and Sagittarius.

Reversed Meaning

When reversed, the Queen of Wands represents the more destructive nature of fire. She may signify a vengeful enemy, jealous lover or domineering friend or relation. She cannot allow others the freedom she seeks for herself, and as a consequence often behaves in possessive and manipulative ways.

As a colleague or business partner, the person represented by this card is unreliable, making empty promises or changing her tactics on a whim. She is unstable, demanding and easily offended.

Abstract Meaning

As an abstract card, the Queen of Wands is closely connected with nature, the countryside and all pleasures linked to wide open spaces. She can also denote altruism, charities, voluntary work and fund-raising ventures – usually connected with the arts or housing organizations. In a general sense, the Queen of Wands signifies success for women, especially when the subject of a reading is female.

KING OF WANDS

KEYWORDS
UPRIGHT: Trustworthy • Vibrant • Passionate
REVERSED: Ruthless • Selfish

TRADITIONALLY, THIS CARD REPRESENTS A MAN WHO IS CONNECTED WITH TRAVEL AND SPECULATIVE VENTURES.

Symbolism of the Card

The King of Wands is depicted on this card as a fiery jinnee, a spirit of fire. His companion is a dragon, symbolic here of power and kingship, and of the marriage of spirit and matter which is the eternal quest of the suit of Wands. When combined, these figures emphasize the links between intuition, which is fire's attribute, and visible power in the external world.

Upright Meaning

The King of Wands, chief masculine spirit of the fire kingdom, is linked with the astrological signs of Aries, Leo and Sagittarius. Typically, he is vital, freedom-loving, ambitious and humorous.

His companion, the dragon, symbolizes his power and connects him with Celtic myth. 'Pendragon', a name associated with the legendary King Arthur, is the Celtic word for 'chief'. This figure represents a man who is often successful in business life, or whom you may meet through your work, financial speculations, any area connected with negotiations, or buying and selling.

As a colleague, this person is trustworthy, innovative and energetic. He is lively and amusing in both work and social settings. He often inspires others and is a gifted manager, boss or team leader.

Romantically, the King of Wands plays two roles. As a partner or potential lover, he is attractive, generous and uplifting company. His volatile vitality is very seductive, and he enjoys the intensity of intimacy. His love of freedom may manifest in a lifelong enjoyment of the countryside – indeed, wide open spaces are important to him in every way, intellectually, spiritually and emotionally.

The King of Wands can also denote the male lover in a clandestine or illicit affair. The Lovers, reversed, would confirm this meaning, or the Three of Swords could symbolize a love triangle. Always charming, often magnetic, the King of Wands should not be taken seriously under such circumstances. Anyone who does so is liable to get badly burned emotionally.

Reversed Meaning

When reversed, the King of Wands typifies the most selfish, ruthless qualities of fire. He can denote a manipulative business contact who will use you as long as it serves his purpose. He may be a rival, competitor or unscrupulous opponent. In love, he represents a delightful flirtation that could wreak emotional havoc. He is only suitable for limited liaisons, holiday romances or delicious, but brief, encounters. His flames are bright and warm but soon die down. Seek enduring sources of warmth elsewhere.

Abstract Meaning

As an abstract concept, the King of Wands denotes property settlements, prenuptial agreements and financial negotiations connected with both marriage and divorce. Charities, trusts, philanthropic organizations and bodies that finance the arts are also symbolized by this card. Negotiations and financial windfalls may also be indicated, especially when other cards amplify this meaning.

THE SUIT OF PENTACLES

The second suit of the Minor Arcana is Pentacles, which embodies the energies of the earth. Where Wands conceive, Pentacles consolidate and preserve. Pentacles are linked with the earth signs of the zodiac – Taurus, Virgo and Capricorn – and share their symbolic qualities of grounded action, practicality and patience. They represent support and all structures on the inner and outer planes – from the foundations of buildings to the organization of productive daily routines. These qualities are crucial for visible success and lasting achievement. The five senses and their individual pleasures are also ruled by this suit.

Resonance and Dissonance – What to Look for

All suits of the Minor Arcana are strengthened or weakened by their companions. This is called resonance and dissonance. Some suits bring out the best in each other, others reduce one another's effectiveness. The suit of Pentacles, like Wands, is objective. Cards from this suit tend to denote tangible, material events, objects and circumstances. The supportive, feminine qualities of earth are enhanced in the presence of Wands. This combination symbolizes practical energy, realistic goals and the necessary grit and determination to fulfil dreams.

When paired with several Swords, Pentacles are weakened. Thinking and theorizing, both represented by Swords, diminishes or undermines practical action – the result is stagnation, inertia. Neutral energies prevail when Pentacles are accompanied by Cups, rulers of emotion. Pentacles offer the soft feelings of Cups some practical armour, while nurturing creative and spiritual dreams with tangible results.

Traditional Areas of Influence

The suit of Pentacles as a whole, and when predominating in a spread, represents these spheres of life:
• Physical reality, the five senses and their associated pleasures.
• Worldly concerns of all kinds – money, earnings, property symbolizing the home or a long-term investment (as opposed to speculative property ventures ruled by Wands). Daily routine work, physical work for gain or pleasure, such as gardening, decorating, cleaning, and so on. Individual status, whether within a relationship, family group, business or community. All issues involving practical commitments, whatever their nature.
• A salty, realistic wisdom born of experience. To preserve what has been gained, to consolidate matters and to support with the enduring love of all earth goddesses is the domain of this sensual suit.

ACE OF PENTACLES

KEYWORDS
UPRIGHT: Prosperity • Practical pleasures
REVERSED: Greed • Financial loss

Symbolism of the Card

The Ace of Pentacles depicts a large disc, coin or pentacle supported by two foliate cows, and surrounded by the fruits and flowers of earthy fertility. The glyphs for the three earth signs of the zodiac, Taurus, Virgo and Capricorn, appear above the pentacle. This Ace connects earthly pleasures and abundance with new beginnings.

Upright Meaning

The Ace of Pentacles heralds the start of a new phase in material or practical affairs. As the Ace of Coins, its other title, it is concerned with cash, earnings, resources and material gain of all kinds. The foliate cows on this sensual card symbolize the goddess as earth mother. They also signify pleasure and nourishment. They are linked with Egyptian Hathor, goddess of love, dance and the dead. She fed the souls of the dead with life-giving milk.

Practical, tangible manifestations may be expected when this card appears in a spread. Frequently, this Ace indicates financial improvements of every kind. As a card of new beginnings, it often represents a good financial contract, and may confirm a career change if the other cards agree.

As an earthy card, this Ace is associated with practical achievements. These activities offer pleasure and potential profit when the surrounding cards support this.

When appearing in an emotional context, this earthy Ace stands for security, permanence and joyful peace. Any relationship is likely to endure, nourish and support you at this time. Sometimes, this card represents a marriage but other cards, such as the Empress or Two of Cups, are necessary to confirm this.

Reversed Meaning

When reversed, the Ace of Pentacles chiefly signifies financial loss through unwise investments, or foolish speculations prompted by greed. The saying 'love of money is the root of all evil' applies to this card reversed. Greed and acquisition for the sake of status and power alone are suggested. In extreme examples, fraud, embezzlement and sharp practices are revealed.

TWO OF PENTACLES

KEYWORDS

UPRIGHT: **Balancing resources**
REVERSED: **Fluctuation • Imbalance**

Symbolism of the Card

This card connects the practical, earthly realm of the suit of Pentacles with the idea of union, balance and harmony, which are the symbolic meanings of the number two. We see a figure holding a large disc in each hand, weighing them up and trying to achieve a balance.

career or secondary skill that could increase your income. Finally, the Two of Pentacles can indicate restlessness, referring to inner balance, a need to channel and focus your energies, so that you have enough time to spare for both your work and your private life.

Upright Meaning

In a reading, the Two of Pentacles suggests the need to achieve some balance in life. This may be between two jobs, or the card may simply describe a self-employed person who is for ever trying to juggle a number of demanding clients or commitments.

Fluctuating finances are often indicated by this card, but the emphasis is on ups and downs – not poverty or severe lack. Practical help or an intriguing offer is sometimes suggested by this card, especially if it is accompanied by a court card representing a person, or an Ace representing a new beginning. In this case, you will be offered an opportunity to develop a part-time

Reversed Meaning

Imbalanced resources are signified by the Two of Pentacles reversed. These may appear as debts, foolish extravagance or 'burning the candle at both ends' and wasting your physical health and energy. When describing a person, the card indicates a moody individual who tends to swing between two extremes, rarely achieving balance.

Generally, this card reversed will suggest inconsistency, lack of purpose and fluctuating fortunes. Negative duality, which lies at the heart of this card, denotes an inability to set clear goals and pursue them. Self-discipline, vision and possibly practical help are all needed at the moment to enable you to overcome this minor obstacle to progress.

THREE OF PENTACLES

KEYWORDS
UPRIGHT: Increase • Praise • Comfort
REVERSED: Halted progress • Limited potential

Symbolism of the Card

The Three of Pentacles shows a figure standing on one pentacle, holding the other two aloft. This downward-pointing triangle of pentacles symbolizes the earth, the natural world, the matrix from which the increase, signified by the card's number three, unfolds.

Upright Meaning

The Three of Pentacles is the card of the builder, craftsman and of practical creativity. It symbolizes increase, whether financial or in terms of attention and praise, because what was begun by the Ace, and balanced by the Two of Pentacles, is now established enough to grow and develop. For this reason, the Three of Pentacles signifies building upon established efforts. Business and creative projects, building good contacts, even professional training – any or all of these precede the success that this card brings. They are the matrix that is devoted to nourishing progress. Now, the bud is ready to flower, the fruit ripens, and the symbolic harvest begins.

When describing your career, this card represents praise, recognition, affirmation of your skills and usually signifies modest material gains as well. The increase it suggests encourages further efforts, acting as a spur to achievement and self-development. When it refers to questions connected with the home and domestic life, the Three of Pentacles relates to increased comfort, decorating, building work and all home improvements.

Reversed Meaning

There are many different factors that temporarily prevent or delay success. The Three of Pentacles reversed denotes fear, lack of direction, lack of effort and inflexibility. Any or all of these factors are holding you back. Since this is an earthy card, it can indicate a great love of security. Again, fear of risk-taking is blocking creative impulses and denying you the opportunity to develop your full potential. When signifying others, this card warns of mean employers or penny-pinching clients. Do not hope for generosity or rewards in the immediate future, as they will not be forthcoming.

FOUR OF PENTACLES

KEYWORDS
UPRIGHT: Improved security
REVERSED: Avarice • Misers

Symbolism of the Card

The Four of Pentacles shows an X-shaped figure bestriding two pentacles while holding two more aloft. This shape symbolizes the double foundation inherent in this card, whose number is four and whose element is earth. X traditionally symbolizes male and female, active and passive, phallic mountain and feminine cave.

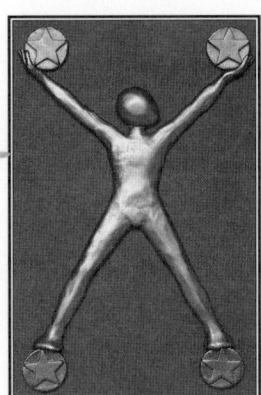

Upright Meaning

This card suggests financial improvements that increase your security and comfort. It suggests a firm foundation in the material world and, although it is not indicative of vast riches, it promises improved material circumstances.

When its position suggests work or career issues, this card signifies a consolidation of responsibility, power or status. Financial gain often accompanies these but is slow and steady. Lasting increase over a period of time is represented here, not the bonuses or windfalls sometimes heralded by the Three of Pentacles.

When signifying a person – again, the position in a spread will help you here – this card represents someone who is overly impressed by position, status symbols or wealth. Such people tend to be social climbers with shallow values and suspect loyalties.

Reversed Meaning

When the Four of Pentacles is reversed it indicates an obsession with money. It represents an uneasy blend of avarice, envy and dissatisfaction. No matter how much money this person has, it is never enough to share. The material world and all its pleasures have become tainted by an appetite that is for ever unsatisfied.

When supported by positive cards, the Four of Pentacles reversed reveals financial anxiety, financial burdens and thoughts of lack in general. This, in turn, represents the limitations of all the fours, for such fears are draining energy, blocking progress and also tarnishing joy. Whether a phase or an habitual attitude, it is imprisoning the individual. Damaging fears should be dealt with as soon as possible in order to avoid lasting difficulties. Buy a big bunch of roses today!

THE MINOR ARCANA

FIVE OF PENTACLES

KEYWORDS

UPRIGHT: Loss • Lack • The outcast
REVERSED: Faith restored

Symbolism of the Card

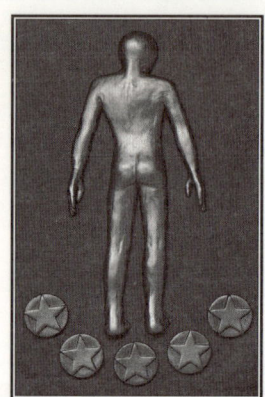

A despondent figure stands alone, facing away from five pentacles. The conflict and strife, represented by five, is manifesting in the material world, symbolized by the suit of Pentacles. The battle is for spiritual riches, but its opening moves are often performed on the battlefield of financial well-being.

Upright Meaning

The Five of Pentacles is the card of the outcast, the unloved, the insolvent. This can manifest on many levels, sometimes psychologically, sometimes materially. The essential meaning of this card, at its most straightforward, is poverty, financial loss and hardship. Nearby cards will reveal the reason for this. Since five is an unstable number, signifying change, it does not represent a permanent condition; merely one that is difficult, disheartening and seemingly endless.

A sense of loss and lack pervades the spirit when this card appears. Optimism and energy may be in short supply now, faith is lost and dreams hard to come by. And this is the true conflict signified by the Five of Pentacles – the battle between the forces of growth and stagnation. The healing powers of hope and the regenerative qualities of self-love are sorely needed to inspire victory. An intimate analysis of the surrounding cards is crucial, for they will suggest remedies and reveal the passing nature of this cloud of doubt and uncertainty. Ultimately, this card has much in common with the nigredo of the alchemists – a dense process necessary for the transformation of base metal into true gold.

Reversed Meaning

The Five of Pentacles reversed restores hope, faith and finances. Help is now available – perhaps through contacts, a grant or bursary, or rewards for hard work that has been undertaken in the past. Spiritual growth, an optimistic attitude and a sense of progress are springing up like flowers in the desert. A candle always burns most brightly in the dark; a challenging experience has served its purpose and you can now make good.

SIX OF PENTACLES

KEYWORDS
UPRIGHT: Generosity • Abundant benefits
REVERSED: Theft • Financial constriction

Symbolism of the Card

The Six of Pentacles is depicted as an upward-pointing pyramid or triangle of coins, enclosed by two curving ribbons. The pyramid is a masculine, solar symbol, emblematic of worldly action. It combines with the feminine qualities of the number six to symbolize harmony and flow in the material world denoted by the suit of Pentacles.

Upright Meaning

The Six of Pentacles is, traditionally, the card of philanthropy, generosity and valuable gifts. Abundance and benefits may be given or received, for this card marries both active and receptive impulses. The surrounding cards will indicate whether this card represents gifts received or gifts bestowed on others.

While cash, in the form of unearned income, bursaries, legacies or grants is often signified, the Six of Pentacles also represents practical help of various kinds. Your path is smoothed and your progress aided by a powerful individual, an established organization or a charitable institution. You could be offered clients, introductions, an interest-free loan, a free workspace or some equipment. Awards, prizes, enhanced status and worldly power may also be denoted by this card. If you are in a position to benefit others, this card can refer to the kind of practical help and support you can offer them.

Reversed Meaning

The Six of Pentacles reversed has two distinct meanings, although both are connected with the idea of sacrifice common to all Sixes. It warns against theft, burglary, gambling and extravagance. In this instance, financial sacrifice comes in the form of attack from outside, or foolish behaviour sparked off by some inner compulsion.

Legal financial settlements are also signified by the Six of Pentacles reversed. Such settlements are generally associated with business closure, divorce or dividing up the possessions of the dead. The motif of sacrifice here represents the need to share, perhaps unwillingly, or to let go of the need for total autonomy and freedom in financial affairs.

THE MINOR ARCANA

SEVEN OF PENTACLES

KEYWORDS

UPRIGHT: Seed-time • Unknown possibilities
REVERSED: Reinvention • Change through risk

Symbolism of the Card

The Seven of Pentacles depicts seven pentacles flanked by two germinating seeds. These seeds express potential; they have sprouted but have yet to develop. Seven, a mutable feminine number, represents change and the discovery of unconscious gifts and directions. Here, this manifests through the earthy world of the suit of Pentacles.

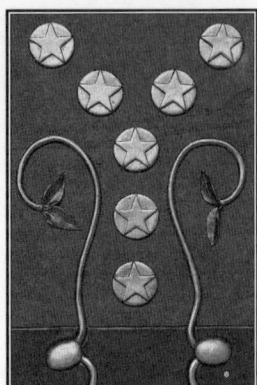

Upright Meaning

This card is linked with hard work that is currently producing little financial gain. The temptation is to allow anxiety to block progress. Fears of poverty and unfounded concerns about the future may subvert energy and creative growth at this time. Focusing on the rewards, instead of the process required to claim them, could be the problem.

When presented in a positive, constructive context, the Seven of Pentacles denotes the sustained effort and concentration needed at the beginning of any venture or project. These include both paid and unpaid work. Voluntary work, parenting and serious hobbies will also require attention and energy at the moment.

Traditionally, this is the farmer's card. It offers you this analogy: to grow a healthy crop requires preparation – the ground must be cleared, fertilized and made ready to receive the seeds. The more thorough your preparation, the better the crop may be. But the seeds must germinate in their own time; you cannot control this process, only ensure the best possible conditions. Your projects or career direction are at the same stage. Be patient, deal with groundless fears and imaginary enemies of progress and you will be productive.

Reversed Meaning

A sense of wasted effort, disillusion and disappointment marks out a rather dull and depressing phase in life. However, since all Sevens contain the energy of change, this chapter is about to come to an end. Attitudes and beliefs about work, creativity and money will undergo a major shake-up: it is time to abandon your old ideas and behaviour, weed your patch and begin anew.

EIGHT OF PENTACLES

KEYWORDS
UPRIGHT: Prudence • Education • Skills
REVERSED: Restriction at work • Loss of direction

Symbolism of the Card

Eight pentacles are laid out across the pages of a book. A ribbon marks the place. The book represents education and the ribbon symbolizes energy. Eight, a powerful number denoting fate and structure, is here connected with the actions that make up each person's own story.

Upright Meaning

The Eight of Pentacles is the card of the apprentice, student and seeker after knowledge and wisdom. In worldly terms, it often signifies short courses, the development of work-related skills, training and the expansion of knowledge for practical gain. Here, you are able to enlarge and expand your skills so you become more effective. This card denotes opportunities for you to strengthen and improve the structures in your life.

The doubts and confusions of the Seven of Pentacles have now given way to the clarity and sense of purpose inherent in this sober, industrious card. The creation of new structures, or the enhancement of existing ones, is now necessary if the renewal and rewards symbolized by the Nine, which follows, are to be fully enjoyed. It is time for practical progress and application. There is a quiet sense of excitement too, as the challenge of developing your abilities is met and you feel yourself slowly moving forward. Financially, this card denotes small, regular savings plans, care with resources, and sometimes modest cash gifts.

Reversed Meaning

Sometimes restriction and sacrifice are symbolized by the Eights. In this instance, you may be limited at work or by the kind of work you do. A refusal to develop your skills may be to blame, or the problem could be a misuse of your abilities or difficulty in expanding them. It is time to ask yourself whether you are in the right job, or why you are unemployed, and what you might do to change and dissolve these restrictions. Occasionally, dishonesty and minor fraud are symbolized by this card – misuse of intelligence is then signified, but this will be affirmed by other cards.

NINE OF PENTACLES

KEYWORDS
UPRIGHT: Material pleasures • Gain
REVERSED: Temporary loss • Illegal earnings

Symbolism of the Card

This card is presented as a symbolic plant bearing ripe fruits, emblematic of abundance. Completion of a cycle, denoted by the number nine, is achieved in the material world. Its fruits, the results of the cycle just gone, manifest in the world of matter as cash or pleasures. material, and expresses its inner joy through luxuries, new clothes, new furniture, treats and gifts. The table is laid out for a feast, piled high with ripe fruits and decked with flowers. You may accept this invitation because it comes from a benevolent, overflowing source. It is time to receive the gifts of the cosmos with grace and pleasure.

Upright Meaning

The Nine of Pentacles is a supremely sensual card, denoting unabashed pleasure and a sense of abundance which may, or may not, be related to actual material circumstances. At its most basic and mundane, this is the card of easy money, windfalls, wins, cash benefits and unearned income. It differs from the Six of Pentacles, which carries the underlying theme of charity and the generosity of others. This card, as the end of a practical, material cycle, has more in common with jackpots, bonanzas and unexpected largesse.

When closely connected, either by position or companion cards, with your emotional world, it signifies taking pleasure in the senses. The suit of Pentacles is objective and

Reversed Meaning

When the Nine of Pentacles is reversed it symbolizes insecurity, material loss and lack of resources. Generally, these affect established business ventures, property deals, home improvements and expansive practical plans of every type. As the end of a cycle, however, this must be interpreted as a temporary phase requiring changes. Cut out the dead wood, salvage whatever is viable and plan for the future. The other meaning of this card is illegal earnings, undeclared income, cash sums that are unaccounted for or 'creative accounting'. This card's position and the supporting cards should be analysed carefully before selecting your precise interpretation.

TEN OF PENTACLES

KEYWORDS

UPRIGHT: Family matters • Prosperity • Ease
REVERSED: Burdens • Retirement • Restriction

Symbolism of the Card

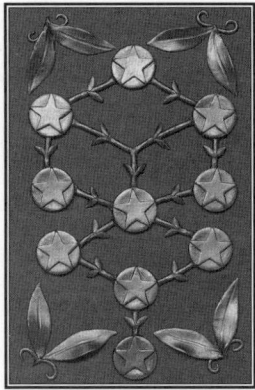

The Ten of Pentacles is presented on the cabbalistic Tree of Life, representing culmination, endings and new beginnings. The design symbolizes nourishment, raw materials and spiritual connections between the world of matter and the energies of the unseen realms.

these sums of money are one-off payments.

When this meaning seems totally unlikely, the Ten of Pentacles simply represents a pinnacle of prosperity. A new start can be created by investment, by using material security to explore new options, or by developing creatively and spiritually.

Upright Meaning

The Ten of Pentacles, as its design suggests, symbolizes a culmination in the material world, and simultaneously represents the ending of one particular phase in life and the start of a new one. The card is linked to families and their assets. In a reading, this meaning must be carefully interpreted for it can be very subtle.

At its simplest, the card augurs an inheritance, financial help or practical benefit from your family. It can also mean that you will be able to benefit your family in some practical way, since its core meaning is prosperity. It denotes lump sums from property sales, stocks and shares, tax windfalls, insurance policies, trust funds and so on. As a Ten, representing the end of a cycle,

Reversed Meaning

The Ten of Pentacles reversed symbolizes practical restrictions. These may come through early retirement, through relatives or through simple financial misfortune – usually connected with official authorities such as governments, utilities or tax collectors. When indicating burdens imposed by the family, other cards will clarify how this may manifest. When accompanied by the Hierophant, for example, it would point to family burdens of a religious or status-conscious nature. Care of the elderly or infirm, demanding relatives, anxieties and energy drains of this type can be denoted. The Eight of Swords is another card to look for. It suggests that a new attitude to this problem might be needed.

PAGE~PRINCESS OF PENTACLES

KEYWORDS
UPRIGHT: Happiness • Comfort
REVERSED: Lack of information and resources

Symbolism of the Card

Here, the Page~Princess of Pentacles holds his or her symbolic disc protectively, symbolizing one of the overriding qualities of the element of earth, and of the suit itself. Strawberry plants in fruit and flower signify sweetness of spirit and the innocent energy of this Page. Two feline creatures with lunar shells sleep beneath the Page~Princess, representing the gentle, comfortable nature of this card.

Upright Meaning

When signifying a child of either sex, the Page of Pentacles represents a loving, unimaginative, good-natured individual. The earth signs of Taurus, Virgo and Capricorn may feature prominently, too, although this is not always the case. Children with weight problems are often denoted by this card, as are those with eating disorders.

Reversed Meaning

When it is reversed, the Page of Pentacles denotes a painfully shy child who finds it almost impossible to communicate well. Stubborn, silent children may be represented, or perhaps those who are unable to make friends easily.

Abstract Meaning

In its most general sense, this card suggests happy news concerning a family member, close friend or child. When the news seems to be strictly personal, it will concern money matters, property or home issues, investments and small windfalls or gifts. Sometimes it denotes an offer of work, although usually it is something to keep you going rather than a spectacular career move. Small loans, or even finding a little money, may be signified too.

When it appears reversed in a spread, the Page~Princess of Pentacles means unexpected financial or material loss – again, nothing major is indicated, but you may have to pay some extra bills, there could be the loss of some money through carelessness or the theft of a wallet or purse.

KNIGHT OF PENTACLES

KEYWORDS
UPRIGHT: Stoical • Ambitious • Honest
REVERSED: Low self-esteem • Limitations

Symbolism of the Card

The Knight of Pentacles gazes at the symbol for his suit as if assessing its potential – signifying the ambitious qualities of this masculine spirit of earth. Acorns and oak leaves suggest his staying power and ability to bring things to fruition slowly but surely, just as the oak takes a great many years to reach its full size and potential. Two cat-like creatures gaze out from the base of the card.

Upright Meaning

When signifying a person, the Knight of Pentacles represents a young man with patience and quiet ambition. He is hard-working, determined and often rather conservative in his opinions, outlook and behaviour. He can, in fact, make dull company for he is rarely witty or spontaneous. However, beneath this rather respectable veneer he is – like all the Pentacles – sensual, passionate and steadfast. Such qualities, like the mineral wealth of the earth itself, are buried beneath the surface and need skill and perception to uncover them. He is a loyal friend, a stable romantic partner and a reliable workmate who is unfazed by stress or other unfavourable circumstances.

Reversed Meaning

Reversed, the Knight of Pentacles signifies a young man struggling against financial difficulties or career problems. Sometimes it simply denotes someone who is currently unemployed or who has lost their way a little and does not know what to do next.

Abstract Meaning

As a herald or messenger card, the Knight of Pentacles represents goals, dreams and the practical steps you must take towards making these come true. He is a positive emblem of healthy ambition and the ability to work tirelessly towards achieving it. Small savings, investments and loans relating to your work or career may also be denoted. When the Knight of Pentacles is reversed, there may be difficulties with loans, credit arrangements and personal finances. This is not a good time to borrow money or to make any long-term financial commitments.

THE MINOR ARCANA

QUEEN OF PENTACLES

KEYWORDS
UPRIGHT: Practical • Sympathetic • Pleasure-loving
REVERSED: Self-centred • Avaricious

TRADITIONALLY, THIS CARD REPRESENTS A WOMAN WHO IS CONNECTED WITH TRADITION, STRUCTURES AND ASSETS.

Symbolism of the Card

The Queen of Pentacles rises from her leafy bed, holding a pentacle and admiring a rose in full bloom. The Queen's deep affinity with all natural things is symbolized both by the flower that she holds and by the ripe strawberries that adorn the two upper corners of the card. Two foliate cows sleep peacefully beneath her sensual image, embodying her fertile femininity.

Upright Meaning

This card is emblematic of earthy womanhood and has close links with the earth signs of the zodiac – Taurus, Virgo and Capricorn. The Queen resonates with the ancient goddesses of hearth and home, with the guardian spirits of the home, and with goddesses of marriage, such as Greek Hera and Roman Juno. Her other mythic links are with the fertile mother figures of every pantheon, who embodied the earth itself. Her compassion for others finds practical outlets: she is likely to cook for you, offer you a lift, help you move into a new home, give sensible, down-to-earth advice. She is often deeply sympathetic and supportive but rarely offers purely emotional support, preferring the motto 'actions speak louder than words'.

She loves sensual luxuries – fresh flowers, elegant designs, good food – a whole range of pleasures. This woman often works hard in order to indulge her tastes; since she is astute and stoical in her pursuit of success she frequently achieves her goals. As a colleague or business associate she is well-organized, patient and pragmatic. She does not object to unglamorous routine tasks if she can see a final result or if she feels that she is gradually improving her circumstances.

As a lover, the Queen of Pentacles is *warm*, tactile, loyal and steady. Rarely impulsive in love, she prefers a stable partnership with someone who is financially secure – or at least solvent. She admires ambition and drive, but perversely may devote herself to a series of 'lame ducks' in the hopes of transforming them into swans. She is then often bitterly disappointed, and pours her energy into supporting the relationship single-handed. Letting go is difficult for her, because she is slow to commit herself and regards each relationship as an investment.

Reversed Meaning

Reversed, the behaviour, emotions and values of the Queen of Pentacles are dominated by her need for security. Her pleasure-loving extravagance becomes selfish and greedy, her ambitious streak hardens into something resembling obsession. She focuses on herself at the expense of everyone else, and will ruthlessly use others to further her aims. Emotionally, she is only interested in those who have status, wealth or influence – she may marry solely for material comfort and be numb to love and desire. As a colleague, she may be a workaholic or ruthless competitor. While lacking the manipulative qualities of the Queen of Cups, or the sharp wit of the Queen of Swords, nonetheless she makes a dogged opponent with a heart of stone.

Abstract Meaning

Luxuries, indulgences, gifts and treats are all represented by the Queen of Pentacles as an abstract card, with a special emphasis on sensual pleasures such as soft fabrics, perfumes, beauty treatments and gourmet foods. She may indicate the need for some small pleasures, something to expand your everyday experience and excite your senses. When reversed, this card warns against limitation, against a tight-fisted attitude towards life, love and money. You will not lose anything by sharing yourself, or your good fortune, with others.

THE MINOR ARCANA

KING OF PENTACLES

KEYWORDS

UPRIGHT: **Steadfast** • **Sensual** • **Productive**
REVERSED: **Domineering** • **Predictable**

TRADITIONALLY, THIS CARD REPRESENTS A MAN WHO IS
CONNECTED WITH TRADITION, STRUCTURES AND ASSETS.

Symbolism of the Card

The King of Pentacles is emblematic of the many powers and mysteries of the earth. His enduring qualities are suggested by the foliate cows, plus the oak leaves and acorns. The oak is a sacred tree in many European mythologies, and in Amerindian symbolism it is sacred to the great Earth Mother. Acorns represent fertility and immortal life, and also slow growth and productivity.

Upright Meaning

The King of Pentacles is an earth spirit, linked to the three astrological signs of Taurus, Virgo and Capricorn. In Celtic mythology the oak, whose leaves and fruits accompany this King, was a holy tree sacred to the Creator. For the Druids of northern Europe it stood for the masculine principle, and for the ancient Greeks it had connections with Zeus, king of the gods, and with Philemon as a symbol of marital bliss and devotion. All these fine qualities are embodied in the King of Pentacles at his masculine best. His devotion is steadfast, whether to a lover, a cause or an ambition. Like the oak, he grows slowly but endures, and is capable of standing his ground when things seem to go wrong. His is the faith that can move mountains, and his progress in life proceeds at a steady, measured pace.

In business life the King of Pentacles represents reliability, wealth and security. He often signifies a financially secure man who is building his material world on strong foundations. While rarely inspired to take risks, he is shrewd and astute, and will make sure he sees a project through once he has committed himself to it.

Romantically, the King of Pentacles is in many ways an ideal partner. He is sensual, tactile and capable of deep devotion. His approach may be slow and his need for security makes him cautious, but a strong and passionate heart beats beneath a rather conventional veneer. However, jealousy and possessive behaviour spring from his intensity of spirit, for he does not enjoy ambivalent liaisons, needing to know where he stands in your affections before declaring himself.

Reversed Meaning

When it is reversed, this card can display some of the less attractive characteristics associated with the earth signs. In Chinese symbolism, the oak represents male strength but also stands as a warning to those who cannot bend, like the willow, to accommodate a storm. The oak resists and is therefore damaged by its apparent strength. Obstinate, overbearing and deaf to reason, the reversed King may be his own worst enemy. In relationships his need for security may overwhelm his partner, as he erupts in jealous tantrums and makes impossible demands. In business, his innate caution can turn him into a loser who misses opportunities through fear of the unknown.

Abstract Meaning

As an abstract symbol, the King of Pentacles represents large, successful, traditional and established organizations – and the professions that support them, such as the law, banking, the Stock Exchange and property management. On a more personal note, this card denotes the growth of a business, the mastery of a profession or the gradual movement towards a long-held ambition or goal. Generally, this card suggests improved material circumstances, increased earning power and material comfort. When negative (either reversed or accompanied by challenging cards), the King of Pentacles warns against insufficient funds, lack of financial support for an idea or the closing-down of a business venture.

THE SUIT OF SWORDS

Swords, the third suit of the Minor Arcana, represents the element of air. Its cool, clear energies are linked with the air signs of the zodiac – Gemini, Libra and Aquarius. Like these signs, Swords symbolize mental activity – thought, logic and reason. At its most beneficial, the suit of Swords offers clarity, balance, communication and verbal dexterity. The essence of air is manifest in wit and wordplay, in precise definition, in scientific reasoning, in elegant analysis.

Traditionally, Swords bring discord and strife, trouble, bondage and betrayal. The negative symbolism connected to this suit reflects the power of anxiety, pessimism, self-pity and limited thinking. Swords frequently represent states of mind rather than actual events, conversations rather than actions. When feelings, intuitions or practical considerations are ignored, then thought alone can create unnecessary suffering. Swords are indeed double-edged symbols.

Resonance and Dissonance – What to Look for

All four suits of the Minor Arcana are weakened or strengthened by their companions. This is called resonance and dissonance, and is based upon the elemental and symbolic meanings of each suit of the Minor Arcana. Some combine well and bring out the best in each other, others have little in common and reduce one another's effectiveness when they appear together. The energies of Swords are strengthened – to positive or negative effect – by the presence of Wands and Cups. Wands stimulate Swords, offering energy and inspiration to back up well-thought-out ideas or plans. With the soft, flowing, fertile energy of Cups, Swords symbolize structured creativity. The presence of Pentacles will weaken a group of Swords, denoting a conflict between practical reality and, perhaps, wishful thinking. Impractical ideas or an inability to work with what you have are suggested here.

Traditional Areas of Influence

Each Sword has a specific meaning. But each suit governs its own realm. When Swords predominate in a spread, it will tend to focus on the following:

• Decisions, mental activity of all kinds, intellectual stimulus.
• All forms of verbal or written communication, including libel and slander, public-relations exercises, lies and misinformation.
• The law; science – especially physics and astronomy; mathematics; computer technology; games of logic and mental skill, such as chess; crossword puzzles and word games; feats of memory.

ACE OF SWORDS

KEYWORDS
UPRIGHT: Fate • Power • Justice
REVERSED: Disrupted plans • Cutting the ties

Symbolism of the Card

One silvery sword rises between two winged sylphs and points towards two winged hearts, symbols of the soul. The glyphs for the air signs of the zodiac, Gemini, Libra and Aquarius, affirm the Ace of Swords' connections with the mental realms of this airy suit.

Upright Meaning

The Ace of Swords brings a cool, incisive energy into any reading. It represents the powers of thought and justice, and often signifies a whirlwind of mental energy, ideas and renewed focus and clarity. It can be a card of success and triumph – generally, academic, professional or literary. It has connections with favourable legal judgments, important legal documents and taxation and litigation. Whatever accompanies this card will amplify this interpretation, and it is crucial to assess it in context, since the Ace of Swords represents detached, unemotional energies. Justice may mean a balanced outcome to a dispute, not necessarily the outcome you hope for.

The Ace of Swords is associated with the idea of fate, karma and destiny. This meaning is especially resonant when either the Wheel of Fortune or the World is in the same spread. You are part of a larger, older pattern than you may realize.

As an instrument of change, this card can signify the end of certain patterns in your life. Again, the surrounding cards will tell you what these are. This can be the most exhilarating, powerful Ace of them all, so use its energies wisely.

Reversed Meaning

The power and mental energies that are signified by this card now manifest in your outer life. Stress, power struggles, even quarrels and partings can be denoted. This card cuts through your life, clearing away old ties and connections – sometimes abruptly. Plans are disrupted, typically there are delays to negotiations and anything involving legal processes or financial arrangements. An atmosphere of upheaval may be hard to deal with, but ultimately the changes indicated enable you to make a new beginning.

TWO OF SWORDS

KEYWORDS
UPRIGHT: Tension • Justice • Temporary peace
REVERSED: Release • Troubled peace

Symbolism of the Card

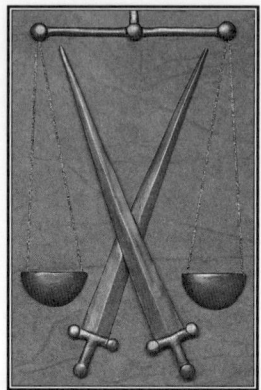

The Two of Swords offers the message of balance, symbolized by the scales of justice in which all facts are weighed and measured. The crossed swords in the centre of the card signify underlying tension. Here, the striving for balance, which is denoted by all the Twos, is manifested in the mental realms.

Upright Meaning

The Two of Swords signifies a kind of ceasefire, a temporary peace, a stalemate or the illusion of stagnation. Beneath apparent inactivity, however, turbulent forces swirl and eddy. A storm is brewing. For the time being, these disruptive forces are kept in check; emotions are repressed, facts suppressed, anger diverted. But look closely and you will see storm clouds gathering on your horizon. Sooner or later the storm will break – bringing lasting peace, dissolving tensions, resolving the situation once and for all. Meanwhile, make use of this calm oasis to gather strength and prepare yourself for the next, more active, phase.

The Two of Swords is linked with Justice in the Major Arcana. As such, it can mean a fair result in any kind of litigation, legal problems, negotiations or conflicts. Justice is on your side, and judgments will be in your favour.

Sometimes, this card describes a person who is unable or unwilling to confront problems for fear of rocking the boat, upsetting the apple cart, or even putting the cat among the proverbial pigeons. The result? Stagnation and loss of progress. The position and context of this card will tell you if this applies to you, your enquirer or someone in love or in business.

Reversed Meaning

Caution is advised when the Two of Swords is reversed. Release from tension or restriction is promised here, but it may be temporary. Do not be tempted to act on impulse; change is in the air but must be introduced gradually. If you are seeking professional advice, take a second opinion. When illuminating an aspect of character, this card warns – as do many of the Swords – of lies, deceit, manipulation and hidden agendas.

THREE OF SWORDS

KEYWORDS
UPRIGHT: Heartache • Catalyst
REVERSED: Heart of darkness

Symbolism of the Card

Three swords are crossed, their pointed tips forming a spiky crown, the whole design suggesting two triangles that represent active and passive energies. Beside them are two hearts, one dark, one light, to show the emotional tensions and challenges symbolized by this disruptive card.

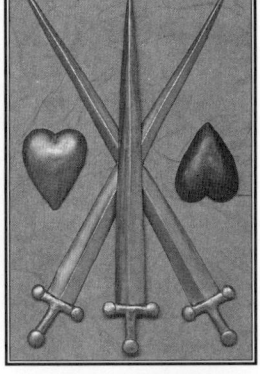

Upright Meaning

The Three of Swords denotes heartache. Because it is an airy, mental card, this emotional pain acts as a catalyst for change, encouraging healing through communication, analysis and change of attitude. Just as strong winds strip dead leaves from autumn trees, this card uses mental tension and confusion to create new growth.

This card has strong traditional associations with love triangles and other lopsided romances. Active obsessions, irresistible temptations and alluring erotic attractions are all signified here. Their essence is fantasy. The love object is a dream figure, a ghostly lover, a god or goddess briefly glimpsed in human shape. For a time, you are under a spell. When the enchantment wears off, as it must, conflict and separation are the result. This is true whether this card describes a clandestine affair or an ongoing, loving relationship.

Tension and conflict may also be present through the need to separate from a beloved partner. It may be that family responsibilities, career issues or study make it necessary for one person to leave the other for a time. This separation also acts as a catalyst for the relationship, moving it on and changing it for the better.

Reversed Meaning

The Three of Swords reversed implies chaos. It represents the anxiety and tension which form the heart of darkness. It is the unfriendly forest of fairytales, the domain of witches, goblins and all the monsters of childhood. But, as in all good stories, the forest is also home to some helpful creatures who can guide you along the paths until you reach home. Heartache exists now, yet healing has already begun. Recovery and rebirth await you.

FOUR OF SWORDS

KEYWORDS
UPRIGHT: Withdrawal • Rest • Convalescence
REVERSED: Exhaustion • Limitation

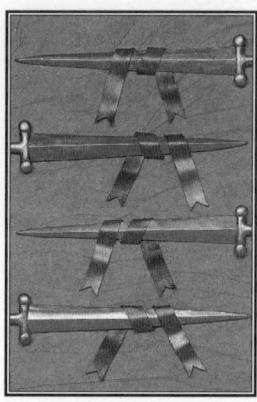

Symbolism of the Card

This card connects the theme of stability and restriction, symbolized by four, with the realm of thought, ruled by this suit. Four swords lie on their sides; they are not in use. They are wrapped in ribbons to show restrained energies, the message of this card. and tension, such as yoga or acupuncture. Mental techniques include meditation and creative visualization. The stability symbolized by this card's number, four, must be found through mental change. Any illness it foretells will be temporary, usually the result of pent-up, long-term stress.

Upright Meaning

The Four of Swords is the card of rest, convalescence and recovery from a mentally stressful phase. It counsels planned withdrawal from everyday life so you may heal and recover your energy. It signifies religious and spiritual retreats, meditation, convalescence and also the need for these things. The mental tension indicated by the Two and Three has reached a peak and needs to be dispersed. It is time for reflection, reassessment and perhaps a gentle change of direction. This meaning is strengthened by the Hermit, the Moon, the World and Temperance.

If your question related to health, then this card can denote minor surgery, investigative procedures or treatments designed to release stress

Reversed Meaning

Nervous exhaustion is the prime meaning of the Four of Swords reversed. This may manifest in actual physical illness, accident or severe energy depletion. The limitations signified by four are being imposed upon you, your need for peace and quiet is being enforced – seemingly from outside. Prolonged stress is generally the cause.

When the surrounding cards agree, the Four of Swords reversed signifies a limited or restricted social life. Friendships and close relationships seem lacklustre, your own response to others is dull and lifeless. Fun and frivolity are hard to find. This is a passing phase, and may help you to focus on the friendships that really matter to you.

FIVE OF SWORDS

KEYWORDS
UPRIGHT: **Separation • Envy • Limitation**
REVERSED: **Defeat • Indecision**

Symbolism of the Card

The Five of Swords shows an interlaced pattern, the points uppermost to symbolize the conflict of all Fives. Four swords are interlocked, denoting limitation, and the fifth stands alone. This central sword lies across a ribbon to signify the separation and broken dreams that are denoted by this difficult card.

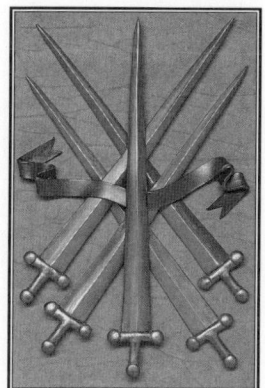

Upright Meaning

All Fives, being unstable numbers, signify the challenges of change. Progress cannot be made without loss, surrender and leaving certain attitudes or routines behind. This, then, is the most difficult kind of change to make, for it demands both submission and loss of control.

When the Five of Swords appears in a spread, it signifies loss, disappointment and apparent failure. Usually this is personal, but sometimes the card suggests that you or your enquirer have caused another person to fail or be disappointed in some way. Such endings bring with them a sense of limitation, or even paranoia. Blame, envy and jealousy may surface – in yourself, or you could be the target of these emotions. A desire to blame someone, or even to suspect malign supernatural forces, can be very strong when this card appears. And indeed, the apparent loss may seem very unfair – the 'winner' in this battle may have used underhand tactics such as gossip, lies and other unpleasant ploys. But, as a card of necessary change, the Five of Swords implies progress. This may be a painful or difficult time, but it opens up new paths and fresh horizons in the long term.

Reversed Meaning

Defeat, plain and simple, is the uncompromising meaning of the Five of Swords reversed. Such loss follows a battle of wits, words, a legal procedure or a negotiation process. There may be bitter feelings and a temporary sense of indecision. 'Where do I go from here?' asks this card. For a short while there is no answer to this question. Concentrate on clearing away the past and recovering balance in your life. The Six of Swords follows this card, promising renewal and restoration.

SIX OF SWORDS

KEYWORDS
UPRIGHT: **Movement** • **Restoration** • **Travel**
REVERSED: **Relief** • **Tenacity**

Symbolism of the Card

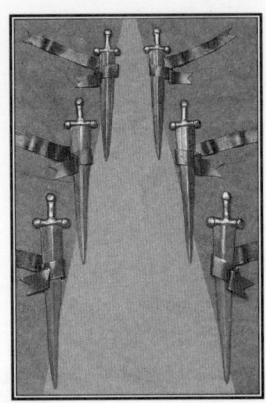

The Six of Swords combines harmony, a quality signified by the number six, with thought, the area of life ruled by the suit of Swords. Six swords, their ribbon banners streaming in the wind, line a straight road which heads into the distance of an unknown future. The road denotes travel and movement, the keys to restoring harmony at this moment.

Upright Meaning

The traditional phrase that best describes the Six of Swords is 'passage away from difficulties'. In this embattled and troubled Minor Arcana suit, tremendous progress has now been made. Peace and harmony are now possible as you move forward into a more contented time. You are leaving behind the disappointments and heartaches symbolized by the Five and Three of Swords, and the tensions and anxieties that are signified by the Two and Four.

This passage is often marked by a real journey, a holiday or pleasure trip. This trip marks the end of a tough time, and its nature will be described by the cards that surround it. Anxiety, worry, stress and depression have generally clouded your life and depleted your energy in the recent past or present. As your circumstances improve, a trip offers you the opportunity to reassess, recover and return with a renewed appetite for life. This card can also suggest that you consider taking a holiday; you may not consciously realize how much you need a change. Travel could be necessary now to broaden the mind and refresh the spirit.

Reversed Meaning

Circumstances continue to present challenges, battles loom ahead and great tenacity is required for one last push. Failure is unlikely, there may even be a temporary peace to look forward to, but the immediate present and future are tough. Yet, overcoming these obstacles is entirely possible and solutions may be suggested by the surrounding cards. It is important not to abandon hope or lose faith at this time. You can win through and can snatch a shining victory from the jaws of defeat.

SEVEN OF SWORDS

KEYWORDS
UPRIGHT: Erratic energy • Theft
REVERSED: Tricks • Superficial communication

Symbolism of the Card

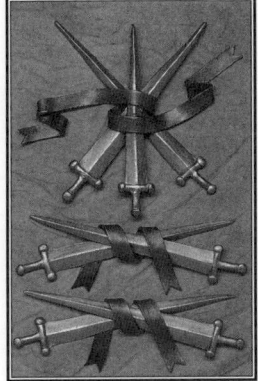

The Seven of Swords links the changeable vibrations of seven with the airy kingdom of Swords, manifesting as changeable mental energies. Seven swords form an intricate pattern, curving ribbons symbolize the ebb and flow of energy at the heart of this unstable card.

Upright Meaning

The Seven of Swords is complex, changeable and contrary. The restless qualities of air, this card's element, combine with the unstable meaning of its number, seven. The message is one of extreme restlessness, agitation and unstoppable change. At its most positive, this card brings a breath of fresh air. Old ideas, routines, assumptions and patterns are challenged; new solutions, wonderful ideas and surprising insights pop up in unexpected ways. It may be difficult to maintain a strict routine but significant progress is made by leaps and bounds – interspersed with times of apparent inactivity. This card often describes a self-employed person whose work flow is variable. When it is negatively presented, the Seven of Swords warns against destructive behaviour, boredom and an inability to commit to long-term plans.

The second meaning of this card is theft. In this instance, its unstable qualities appear in the guise of another person. Rarely, if ever, does this refer to robbery. It warns against the theft of ideas, time and creative energy. Beware of anyone who might betray you, sabotage your plans or undermine your creativity.

Reversed Meaning

When it is reversed, the Seven of Swords means superficial thoughts, whether spoken or written. Meaningless promises, conmen, fast-talking salesmen, anyone who uses words to create a false impression, may be signified by this card. Its position and companion cards will make this clear. If it describes you, by position, its meaning is one of indecision, inability to act and negative thinking. In this case, superficial considerations are masking your intuition and true feelings in some current situation or relationship.

THE MINOR ARCANA

EIGHT OF SWORDS

KEYWORDS
UPRIGHT: Bondage • Mental confusion
REVERSED: Release • Solutions

Symbolism of the Card

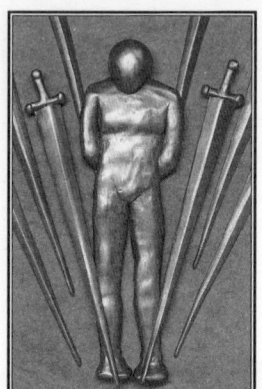

A lonely figure stands, dejected, amidst eight swords. The innate power and strength of the number eight is grounded, because the swords are stuck in the earth – acting as a prison for the figure that they enclose. The Eight of Swords represents blocked mental energy, power that is being held in bondage and a self-created trap.

Upright Meaning

The powerful, assertive energies of the number eight are here turned against the self. Feelings of being trapped, of being alone with insurmountable problems or trapped by negative thoughts, are common when this card appears. It is not possible to see a way out, to arrive at a solution or to escape from this prison at the moment. Fear and indecision have blocked mental energies, and often sap physical energy too. A decision to move forward, to make the progress symbolized by all the Eights, is desirable and necessary. Usually, outside help is needed – a tarot reading could be the first step towards changing the mental patterns that have created the present situation.

Eight is made up of two fours, symbolizing two foundations – one in the physical world and one in the invisible world of the mind and spirit. Balance between mind, body and spirit results in progress – also symbolized by the number eight. Without a firm foundation and a balanced approach, progress is not possible. This card asks you to change your mental habits and patterns so that you may restore your balance, inside and out.

Reversed Meaning

When it is reversed, the Eight of Swords signifies release from restrictions. A difficult phase is ending, solutions have been found and confidence restored. As a relationship card, it indicates quarrels and power struggles within a partnership. One partner would like to dominate the other, and will use negative criticism and other destructive ploys to achieve this. When part of a run of Swords, this card warns against malice and spiteful gossip – the main negative expression of Swords.

NINE OF SWORDS

KEYWORDS
UPRIGHT: Oppression • Despair
REVERSED: Victory over fear

Symbolism of the Card

A vulnerable figure clasps itself protectively as nine swords point, like daggers, towards it. Since nine represents culmination, this pattern may also be interpreted as a sunrise, a symbol of hope and renewal after the troubled night that most of the Swords signify. to heal. There is nothing simple or straightforward about the Nine of Swords, but it does offer hope and underline the need for practical help. Seeking support is the first step towards turning this experience into a new and brighter dawn.

Upright Meaning

Negativity, despair and a feeling of oppression accompany this painful card. Traditionally, it was known as 'the dark night of the soul', a time of grim thoughts. Often the Nine of Swords manifests in the outer world as a recent bereavement, unhappy love affair, broken marriage, or destructive working or home environment. Something you, or the enquirer, is involved with has caused great anguish and misery. This is usually shown by the other cards.

Inner and outer torment are denoted. Disturbed sleep, nightmares, panic attacks and depression may all rob you of energy and purpose. However, all Nines are cards of culmination. It is time to fight back, to overcome suffering and to begin

Reversed Meaning

Fear can be overcome as confidence is regenerated. Optimism triumphs over limitations now, and with renewed hope and faith it will be possible to make a clean break with the past. Emotional repression and an inability to enjoy life may have created difficulties in the recent past or immediate present. As balance is restored, so is the capacity for pleasure, the power of intuition, and the free flow of love and creativity that makes life worth living. Should this card, upright or reversed, indicate some future state, you should be very wary in your interpretation. Remember, Swords is a subjective suit that describes mental states, words, attitudes and opinions. All these are subject to individual perception. Never predict doom and gloom; it is irresponsible.

TEN OF SWORDS

KEYWORDS
UPRIGHT: Darkness before dawn
REVERSED: The enemy within

Symbolism of the Card

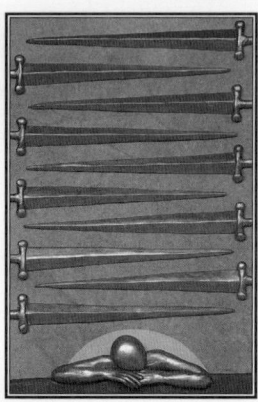

Ten swords fill the design on this card, creating a sense of relentless attack. But the sun is appearing above the horizon, conveying the optimistic message that it is always darkest just before the dawn. The number ten signifies transcendence, creating an overview of the situation rather than presenting you with an impossible challenge. of hidden enemies. However, negative thinking is transformed by the experience, just as the putrefaction stage of alchemy was considered necessary to the end result, the glorious elixir of eternal life. Meanwhile, you should examine all documents with great care, confide in few people and only those you trust, and fine-tune your intuitive antennae. Things, as they say, can only get better from now on.

Upright Meaning

The Ten of Swords is, admittedly, a bleak card signifying ruin and betrayal. This, traditionally, comes through slander, libel, fraud, embezzlement or malicious campaigns designed to discredit an individual or business. As a Ten, it also signifies the ending of a long-term situation – whether a relationship, business interest, career or financial arrangement. And it is because all Tens represent transcendence of some kind that this card is not as gruesome as it might first appear. It really does represent that ageless cliché: 'It's always darkest before the dawn.'

This card may herald a painful or difficult time in your life, or warn

Reversed Meaning

The Ten of Swords reversed denotes the enemy within, the inner saboteur or killjoy who can poison or destroy most things – given half a chance. This ugly creature masquerades as self-pity, low self-esteem, negative beliefs, limitations. Its root cause is fear, and it can be conquered in numerous ways – through positive thinking techniques, visualization, therapy, creative work and love. Its presence in most human beings is eternal, but it need not be allowed to run amok, destroying joy and pleasure. This card suggests that self-awareness and a desire to change can work small miracles.

PAGE~PRINCESS OF SWORDS

KEYWORDS
UPRIGHT: Gossip • News • Ideas
REVERSED: Spite • Sudden disruptions

Symbolism of the Card

The figure on this card stretches up towards two winged hearts that symbolize his or her path towards the pure wisdom of the mature spirit that has transcended material limitations. Two doves flank the Page's tail, signifying messages, news and diplomacy.

Upright Meaning

When this card represents a young boy or girl, it describes a bright, agile and well-coordinated individual. He or she enjoys words, games of mental skill and team sports. When signifying an acquaintance or associate, this card represents verbal diplomacy and negotiation skills. It may denote someone you deal with by phone, fax or otherwise communicate with at a distance. Friendships formed on the Internet, for example, are symbolized by this card, which manifests in the realms of mental excitement and innovation.

Reversed Meaning

The Page of Swords reversed denotes a spiteful person, a vindictive gossip or someone who is spreading misleading or malicious rumours. Spoken or written lies are also suggested when this card appears in a spread – writers of anonymous letters fall into this category, as do con-artists and tricksters of every conceivable type.

Abstract Meaning

News, information, letters, phone calls and communications about change are signified by the Page~Princess of Swords. Whether these are welcome or not will be indicated by the card's position and accompanying cards. When describing the subject of a reading, this Page heralds mental change – usually through improved communication skills, an awakened curiosity, a boost to mental energy or new ways of thinking, learning and researching. Clarification, focus and direction may all be important when this card appears. In a general sense, this card represents talk, gossip, scandal and pleasurable conversations. As always, check the context to decide whether this is positive or negative.

THE MINOR ARCANA

KNIGHT OF SWORDS

KEYWORDS

UPRIGHT: Skilful • Precise • Inventive
REVERSED: Deceitful • Quarrelsome • Aggressive

Symbolism of the Card

The Knight of Swords is shown on this card soaring up towards the horizon, his sword raised, to symbolize his innate energy. Above him, two winged stars signify hope and guidance. Beneath, two doves represent the joyful messenger birds that appear in many ancient mythologies. Here they are emblematic of inspiration, innocence, and the spirit of life and light.

Upright Meaning

When the Knight of Swords denotes a young man, he is intelligent, quick-witted, restless and often inventive. He is articulate and logical, sometimes to his own detriment – for he can discount intuitive guidance because it seems illogical or irrational. He can, however, be impetuous and surprising to others, for he tends to act quickly and with confidence. He may be a student, or work in advertising, public relations, media industries, computers or the music business.

Reversed Meaning

When this card is reversed, the Knight of Swords is deceitful, misleading and treacherous. If he is confronted, he adopts a belligerent attitude or picks a fight to confuse you. He is, needless to say, not to be trusted with information, money or secrets.

Abstract Meaning

When the Knight of Swords is abstract, by spread position or accompanying cards, he brings great energy and movement into your life. He embodies the 'winds of change', which may manifest as inventive plans, new friends, a revolution in routine or lifestyle. The context of this card, and whether it is upright or reversed, will determine whether this metaphorical whirlwind is positive or negative. Unexpected connections are often signified by the Knight of Swords, as are chance encounters. When accompanied by the Six of Cups, he represents the reappearance of a long-lost lover, friend or relation.

THE SUIT OF SWORDS

QUEEN OF SWORDS

KEYWORDS
UPRIGHT: Graceful • Perceptive • Rational
REVERSED: Intolerant • Toxic • Troubled

TRADITIONALLY, THIS CARD REPRESENTS A WOMAN WHO IS CONNECTED WITH COMMUNICATIONS, THE LAW AND SCIENCE.

Symbolism of the Card

The Queen of Swords hovers above a double-headed eagle; winged hearts in each upper corner of the card protect and inspire her. Her two-headed eagle accompanied ancient Hittite goddesses and is an alchemical symbol of male–female mercury – the transformative substance which signifies the potential unity of male and female, active and receptive. This Queen combines cool, logical thought processes with feminine grace and charm.

Upright Meaning

Like the double-headed eagle which accompanies her, the Queen of Swords is a complex figure. Potentially very powerful, she is a potent blend of the rational and idealistic, of logic and charm, detachment and flirtatiousness. She understands the nature of paradox and can readily see both sides of a conflict. The weapons of emotion, manipulation and passion usually fail to seduce her. She bears the sword of truth, justice and mental clarity, and draws her strength from her innate intelligence. Like a bird, she soars above the battle and takes an objective overview of conflict – whether she meets it in business or love. The Byzantines, who were so fond of the double-headed eagle symbol, ruled an empire. They wielded immense power, but loved intricate decoration in art and architecture. This Queen of the airy suit of Swords has much in common with them, blending oriental mystery with a talent for clear communication, fine judgement with her penchant for games and dancing.

The Queen of Swords can also represent an enigma. She, like the High Priestess, can denote an unavailable woman, a fantasy lover, a dream without flesh or substance. She may appear as a clandestine lover in any kind of love triangle. These situations are usually symbolized by the Lovers reversed or the Three of Swords.

In a love triangle, she represents a woman who enjoys deception, loves secrets and mystery, and is perhaps not prepared to devote herself to a full-time relationship.

Finally, the Queen of Swords may simply represent a divorced or widowed woman whose characteristics will be described by other cards. She is the significator for women born under the air signs of Gemini, Libra and Aquarius.

Reversed Meaning

Reversed, the Queen of Swords is a poisonous enemy, spiteful gossip, and toxic friend or lover. She is quick and clever, and may hide her true motives well – appearing charming or even vulnerable. She is dogmatic, intolerant and often very unhappy. However, she needs help rather than pity. She is relatively harmless when signifying a widow, divorcée or a troubled and bitter woman. Her intelligence suggests her eventual recovery.

Abstract Meaning

When abstract by position in a spread, as a card describing career for instance, the Queen of Swords promises success in all intellectual pursuits. Study, examinations, writing, speaking in public, selling and politics are all well-starred by this card. There may be debates, intense business discussions, a battle of wits or a brainstorming session. When negatively aspected or reversed, this card denotes unhappy partnerships, loneliness, jealous gossip or failed examinations.

THE SUIT OF SWORDS

KING OF SWORDS

KEYWORDS
UPRIGHT: Logic • Intelligence • Reason
REVERSED: Vindictive • Scheming

TRADITIONALLY, THIS CARD REPRESENTS A MAN WHO IS
CONNECTED WITH COMMUNICATIONS, THE LAW AND SCIENCE.

Symbolism of the Card

The King of Swords is depicted on this card as a sylph or a winged spirit of the air. His sword symbolizes the powers of reason, and the ability to analyse situations with logic, intelligence and clarity. The iridescent blue eagle that accompanies the King reveals his highest potential; it represents the liberated spirit soaring upwards towards enlightenment. The winged stars in the upper two corners of the card symbolize hope and guidance.

Upright Meaning

As an individual, the airy King of Swords denotes an intelligent, logical man. Traditionally, he is associated with professional life, and as such often represents a lawyer, accountant, surgeon, teacher, psychologist or other expert. The key to this character is communication.

When he is not working with ideas, he is talking about them or absorbing more information from books, television, computers or other sources of knowledge. Above all, he takes pleasure in exercising his mind in conversation, or by setting himself mental challenges in the form of complex games, such as chess or difficult crossword puzzles.

As a friend or colleague this man is lively, often witty, analytical and argumentative. Easily bored, he needs plenty of mental stimulation. His entertaining company can sometimes become exhausting – intuitive or emotional types may recoil from his bright, agile mind and his passion for logic.

As a lover or partner, the King of Swords enjoys flirtation, fantasy and the pursuit of shared ideals. In the early stages, love is a game of imagination and skill, to be played with a light touch and a romantic turn of phrase. He may beguile his beloved with poetry and music, create romantic scenarios or spring imaginative surprises. However, his delight cools, and rapidly turns to panic, when confronted by the darker depths of passion. And, although his flirtatious escapades frequently inspire jealousy, he finds demonstrations of intense emotion difficult and may coldly withdraw from the relationship completely.

Reversed Meaning

The King of Swords reversed has much in common with Machiavelli, the Renaissance philosopher whose name is now synonymous with subtle scheming and the clever manipulation of power.

The King of Swords reversed seeks control and domination but will never resort to physical violence or overt confrontation. The sword he wields is made of words and ideas – he is the master of malicious rumour, harmful innuendo, slander, misleading information and public relations. He may represent an unscrupulous professional or a man who deliberately withholds the information that you seek.

Abstract Meaning

As an abstract symbol, the King of Swords simply represents advice and information – often with legal or financial implications. Whether this advice is positive (upright card) or negative (reversed card), it will be factual rather than emotional in content. To determine the nature and context of the advice, you must look at the cards surrounding the King of Swords.

THE SUIT OF CUPS

The fourth and final suit of the Minor Arcana is the suit of Cups. Cups belong to the kingdom of water, and are linked with the water signs of the zodiac – Cancer, Scorpio and Pisces. The full spectrum of feelings is expressed by this suit, whose feminine, receptive qualities sustain and nourish the soul. Above all, the suit of Cups is associated with love, relationships and creativity. There is a sense of flow, abundance and fulfilment about the suit of Cups – and its characteristic energies are necessary if projects and love connections are to flourish and develop.

Typically, Cups manifest in the personal life, when describing the home as an emotional base rather than as a business investment, and in artistic and creative partnerships. Like Wands, Cups denote intuition. Here, it is based on intense feelings (and sometimes bodily sensations) rather than the visions typically associated with fiery Wands.

Resonance and Dissonance – What to Look for

All suits of the Minor Arcana are weakened or strengthened by their companions. This is called resonance and dissonance, and is based upon the elemental and symbolic meanings of each suit of the Minor Arcana. Some combine well and bring out the best in each other, others have little in common and reduce one another's effectiveness. Receptive, feminine Cups are weakened by the presence of Wands. In this instance, fire evaporates water, turning it into ethereal mist. The powerful emotions of Cups are unstable when dominated by Wands. Swords, however, strengthen Cups when these two suits are paired in a spread. Here, cool logic provides a useful container for boundless emotions. Cups and Pentacles present a neutral energy, combining feeling and creativity with practical action.

Traditional Areas of Influence

When Cups prevail in a spread it will tend to focus on the following:
• Love in all its manifestations – as true friendship, romance, marriage, infatuations, erotic alliances. And also, the love of animals, especially as pets or domestic creatures; the love of home as a spiritual refuge; passions for spiritual disciplines, for music, for art, for beauty and for creative activities.
• Fertility, generosity, abundance – of the mind, body and spirit.
• Creativity involving colour, taste, ambience, subtleties, comfort.
• Clairvoyance, psychic intuitions, hunches, dreams, spiritual guidance, spiritual healing, cleansing and rebalancing techniques, the unseen, and the boundless oceans of the unconscious mind.

ACE OF CUPS

KEYWORDS

UPRIGHT: Renewal • Love • Creativity

REVERSED: Waste • Disappointment

Symbolism of the Card

The Ace of Cups contains the waters of life, love and creative renewal. It is supported by two mermaids, symbolic of the great depths of the unconscious mind. The cup can be identified with the popular medieval fable of the Holy Grail, a magical chalice that could be found at the centre of paradise. The glyphs for the three water signs of the zodiac, Cancer, Scorpio and Pisces, appear above the cup.

Upright Meaning

Each Ace signifies the essence of its suit. This Ace emphasizes the element of water which corresponds to emotion, inspiration, receptivity and fertility. This cup represents flow in several areas of life – creative endeavour, love and spirituality.

When referring to love, this card frequently suggests the beginnings of a deep and intense relationship. There is a mutual opening of the heart which encourages emotional trust and promotes tender feelings. Within an established partnership, this card reveals a deepening of ties.

As an omen of creativity, the Ace of Cups suggests inspiration from your dreams, from beautiful surroundings, from art or from emotional joy and fulfilment. Fertility is at the heart of this card; often the projects or dreams that you have mused about for a long time will begin to come to fruition now because the time is right and you are in harmony with your inner world.

Reversed Meaning

When the Ace of Cups is reversed, its creative waters are spilled. In love, this signifies emotional turmoil and loss. This position can represent emotional repression, infatuation with an unobtainable partner, destructive fantasies of love, and sometimes fruitless obsession. Other Swords, or the presence of the High Priestess reversed, can confirm this.

In creative matters, an empty cup denotes a block. This may be due to repression, fear, lack of energy or emotional stress. Relaxation techniques associated with water may help. Above all, the heart must open to receive once again, overcoming sterility and spiritual hunger.

TWO OF CUPS

KEYWORDS
UPRIGHT: **Union of love and creativity**
REVERSED: **Disharmony • Separation**

Symbolism of the Card

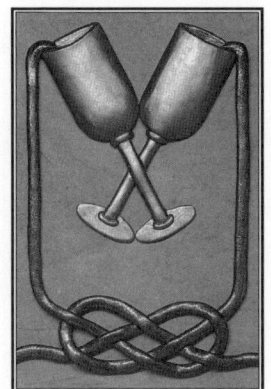

This card expresses the idea of harmony and union within the world of imagination, emotion, feeling and creativity. Two cups are for ever linked by the flow of creative waters between them. This endless knot symbolizes the ever-changing balance of a creative union.

Upright Meaning

The traditional meaning of the Two of Cups is romantic love in its earliest, most idealized moments. It is the moment in every fairytale when Cinderella dances with her prince. But will they live happily ever after? It is not the business of this card to say, for it simply represents a precious moment. If other cards concur, the Two of Cups foretells a romantic interlude that may develop into an important union.

The setting of the Two of Cups is crucial to its correct interpretation. At its heart lies the idea of creative union, and this can often apply to partnerships where artistic and spiritual energies are blended. Fertile working partnerships of all kinds come under the auspices of this card – close friendships in business life, productive and happy teams, the director and actor, the artist and muse – indeed, any situation in which the positive chemistry between individuals creates an energy of its own. And when neither work nor love seem appropriate interpretations, do not forget special friendships and the joys of a meaningful social life.

Reversed Meaning

Imbalanced emotions and lack of harmony are the essence of the Two of Cups reversed. This sense of loss and waste may prompt a separation between partners in love or business. Certainly, the imbalance describes a temporary state of affairs that needs to be resolved in some way. Sometimes this card describes a partnership beset by inequality – one who loves, and one who allows themselves to be loved but offers little in return. Since the Two of Cups warns against wasteful actions, a separation may not be the most positive step to take. The potential for restoring harmony is present but requires effort on both sides.

THE MINOR ARCANA

THREE OF CUPS

KEYWORDS
UPRIGHT: Celebration • Luck • Joy
REVERSED: Extravagance • Indulgence

Symbolism of the Card

The Three of Cups symbolizes the promise of increase and development that is associated with the number three – expressed through the realm of emotions, symbolized by the watery suit of Cups. A joyful, dancing figure holds one cup aloft, celebrating joy, good fortune and vitality. The two cups beside the figure denote abundance.

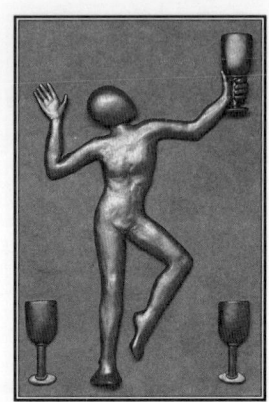

Upright Meaning

The Three of Cups has a special affinity with the Empress of the Major Arcana, for it too carries strong vibrations of fertility and joy. Celebrations of life's turning points are frequently indicated – engagements, weddings, anniversaries, babies and house-warming parties may all be suggested by this card. Indeed, any event that affirms life, joy, luck and love is associated with this happy symbol.

This interpretation expands to include the renewal of health and vitality after a period of low energy; a restoration of pleasure in friendships and social life; the gift of new clothes or jewellery, even if they are from yourself to yourself; prizes and small wins. Above all, this card is infused with a joyful, playful spirit that takes delight in all things, and therefore attracts favour and fortune effortlessly.

Reversed Meaning

Unlike many of the cards in the tarot, the Three of Cups reversed essentially describes the same energies as its upright interpretation. However, it can indicate that the exuberant feelings expressed by this symbol threaten to get out of control. Wild parties; too much delicious food; one glass too many too often ... In the real world, this card warns of weight gain and a sluggish system.

Finances could be put under a strain, too. Habitual extravagance soon depletes resources in all areas. Sometimes the Three of Cups reversed denotes emotional self-indulgence, or suggests that spending too much money is being used to compensate for an emotional hunger and emptiness. Other reversed Cups cards would confirm this interpretation, and so, perhaps, would the presence of the Hermit.

158

FOUR OF CUPS

KEYWORDS
UPRIGHT: **Emotional uncertainty**
REVERSED: **Fear • Stagnation**

Symbolism of the Card

This card symbolizes the ambiguity that results from combining a flowing element, water, with the limitations inherent in four, the number of foundations. A self-protective figure is surrounded by four cups, each of which contains possibilities. Yet the figure is unable or unwilling to stretch out their hands to receive, and so limits themselves.

Upright Meaning

Uncertainty and self-limitation combine in the Four of Cups. A person's creative approach to life, love, work and spiritual exploration has been replaced by a sense of boredom, stagnation and mild depression. A fresh attitude and approach is needed, for although this card is not destructive in itself the attitudes it signifies can block growth and joy.

In love and relationships, the Four of Cups must be assessed in its context. For those who are single it suggests emotional self-protection, springing from difficult experiences and past losses. Such fears rise to the surface when new relationships are possible, and may even destroy the chance of friendship or love before it has the opportunity to develop. Within an ongoing partnership – business or personal – this card warns of boredom that stultifies routine and resistance to change. Each individual must approach this issue in their own way, but the Four of Cups is a gentle wake-up call to the heart, mind and spirit. It urges re-evaluation and a search for fresh inspiration.

Reversed Meaning

Unfounded fears are signified by the Four of Cups reversed. Primarily, these fears centre upon loss of security, whether at work or in a relationship. The terror of being alone may lead to unfulfilling friendships, or superficial, shallow love affairs. Clinging to a relationship that no longer serves either party can be another manifestation of this card. From such fears a sense of futility arises, and life loses its savour. The nature of the fear, and whether it affects work or love, will be clarified by the surrounding cards. New opportunities must be sought now if progress is to be made.

THE MINOR ARCANA

FIVE OF CUPS

KEYWORDS
UPRIGHT: Loss of faith • Hidden treasures
REVERSED: Hope restored

Symbolism of the Card

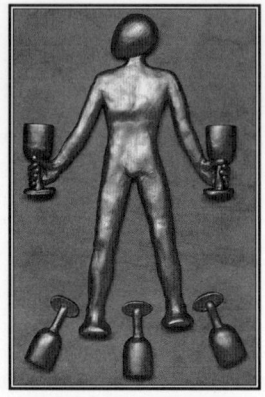

The Five of Cups links five, an unstable, volatile number, with the realms of your secret heart. A figure observes three empty cups, their contents lost or wasted. But two full cups remain, showing that, although something has been lost, there is still something in reserve – some hidden treasures that will offer you hope and progress.

proves to be only human after all. The Five of Cups also describes an imbalanced relationship where one partner feels shut out or lonely because they are not receiving enough love, affection or attention. This may, of course, be an entirely subjective viewpoint – but it will seem real enough to the person enduring the emotional difficulties.

Upright Meaning

This volatile card denotes a time when sadness prevails. Yet this is only temporary, for the card contains the promise of renewal and positive changes. Here, sadness and regret spring from a disappointment in love or the loss of dearly held beliefs and dreams. This card is asking you to release your feelings of despair and reassess your situation. When referring to a relationship, it suggests that, despite present feelings, all is not lost. Two full cups still remain, asking to be explored. Whatever the current crisis, a valuable lesson is contained within it.

Sometimes this card appears when an idealized partner or friend

Reversed Meaning

Five of Cups reversed signifies fresh hope and the return of optimism. Again, the bittersweet flavour of this card influences matters, for it suggests someone has become older and wiser, whatever their age or life-situation. The conclusion of unfinished emotional business is also possible now. A former lover or close friend may return, particularly if the connection ended badly or involved pain and recrimination. Now there is a golden opportunity to set things right, restore harmony and release negative emotions which may have been holding you both back. When this interpretation is appropriate, the Six of Cups will often appear nearby in the spread.

SIX OF CUPS

KEYWORDS
UPRIGHT: Harvesting your history
REVERSED: Negative nostalgia • New beginnings

Symbolism of the Card

The Six of Cups depicts a parent and child encircled by six cups. This symbolizes the child and parent within every individual, situation and endeavour. All things have their roots in the past, and all things need support in order to develop. Six cups promise harmony through effort, linking emotion and creativity with the energies of the number six.

Upright Meaning

The power of the past is the ultimate message of the Six of Cups. Whether remembered or forgotten, valued or despised, your personal history is unique to you. This card suggests that your past is about to play an important part in your future.

When this card appears in connection with love or other close relationships it heralds the return of someone who once meant a great deal to you. Renewal of the relationship may enlarge your life in many ways, through fresh introductions or by inspiring you to develop new interests or talents.

When you are focusing on work or career questions, this card asks you to view your past as a valuable resource. Old contacts could assist you if approached at this time; half-finished projects may yield fresh ideas; past skills might hold the key to future growth and expansion.

If you feel lost or uncertain of your direction, the answer could lie as far back as childhood. What gave you pleasure? What engaged your attention? What did you dream of being or doing? Your past is not haunting you but is offering you a chance to explore your potential.

Reversed Meaning

When nostalgia or regret dominate your actions and thoughts, they act as brakes on your progress. The Six of Cups reversed denotes blockage and possible stagnation springing from an inability to live in the present moment or to move freely into the future. Your memories of past happiness, achievement or even pain and challenge are not serving you now. By whatever means you find appropriate you must close the door firmly on the past and decide to make a fresh start.

SEVEN OF CUPS

KEYWORDS
UPRIGHT: Abundance • Illusions
REVERSED: Deception • Fantasies

Symbolism of the Card

The Seven of Cups is shown in an underwater realm symbolized by a mermaid. She offers up two cups in joyful celebration, while five more cups around her promise abundant potential and choice. This image symbolizes both the dreamy, fairytale qualities associated with the card, and the powerful unconscious energies it represents.

Upright Meaning

The Seven of Cups denotes a time when the boundaries between what is tangible and illusory are blurred or invisible. It describes a time of abundance. However, many of the promises and possibilities before you may be written on the wind. The trick here is to relax and wait until the enchantment wears off before committing yourself to a relationship, a project or any serious choice.

Any attempt to make a firm move will be thwarted. Energy is flowing in all directions; if you try to keep up with it you will simply exhaust yourself. Several potential romantic partners will often appear, or you may be faced with a number of job options or career directions. Such situations test your intuition to the full. The purpose of this time is to reveal the overflowing abundance of the universe. Your true love, or most fulfilling creative direction, will emerge in a little while. Do not seek solidity at the moment because, like fairy gold, it will simply melt away.

Reversed Meaning

When the Seven of Cups is reversed, the message changes, asking you to beware of deceptive delusions. You could be deceiving yourself in some way, perhaps through fantasizing about someone who is unavailable. Other self-induced fantasies may occur through alcohol, drugs or severe procrastination. The dangers of provisional living are highlighted here. If you find yourself constantly making excuses such as 'When I have time', then you must ask yourself how much you really do want your dream. Perhaps it is only a fantasy. This core meaning applies to work, personal and spiritual concerns. It may be time to look again, and to clarify your true dreams.

EIGHT OF CUPS

KEYWORDS
UPRIGHT: **Searching for fulfilment**
REVERSED: **Exhausted emotions**

Symbolism of the Card

The Eight of Cups depicts a pathway lined with cups. Twin streams of liquid flow from the two cups in the foreground, twining this way and that along the road ahead. The pathway on this card symbolizes an emotional and creative journey, while the serpentine pattern of liquid denotes the ebbing and flowing of feelings along the way.

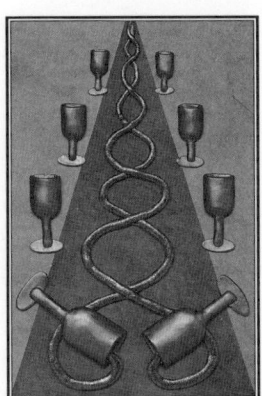

Upright Meaning

Movement and progress are linked with all the cards that belong to the eight vibration. In this card, movement is the result of an emotional impulse, and can also imply leaving something that was once precious. Relationships, long-held ambitions, the yearning for worldly success – these may have disappointed you. What seemed to offer fulfilment has failed to bring happiness, and now you want to move on. As an emotional card, these feelings may, or may not, be realistic. The surrounding cards should add detail, placing these feelings in their correct context.

At its most straightforward, the Eight of Cups describes a journey or period of travel. Visiting other countries and cultures may be a way of searching for meaning in life, or of expanding experience. Either way, this card suggests an underlying restlessness and need for change.

When placed in an emotional context, the card denotes a time when you realize that a relationship or creative project has fulfilled its purpose. This is true whether you are the one who walks away or who experiences rejection. Something must end to make room for something new. Events connected with this card will seem strangely inevitable, for all Eights are linked to the concept of karma and destiny.

Reversed Meaning

Physical and emotional exhaustion are symbolized by the Eight of Cups reversed. This may manifest in inertia, depression, confusion or melancholy. These symptoms may spring from simple physical neglect – poor diet, lack of sleep and exercise – or result from an emotional disappointment. Either way, help and support are needed to restore energy.

THE MINOR ARCANA

NINE OF CUPS

KEYWORDS
UPRIGHT: Satisfaction • Dreams come true
REVERSED: Arrogance • Complacency

Symbolism of the Card

A radiant circle of nine cups surrounds a heart, symbolizing the joyful energies suggested by this lovely card. The circle represents the end of a cycle and is also a symbol of life's eternal cycles. The heart is an emblem of love, the highest emotion associated with this suit. will be washed away by loving feelings and tender affection.

There could be a peak in creative or spiritual development. Dreams may come true, inspiration flows and there is a sense of connection with all of nature. The kind of focused energy needed to to be creative is present, enabling you to overcome obstacles in your path with grace and ease.

Upright Meaning

Joyful, life-enhancing energies are expressed by this card. The end of a cycle has been reached. In this instance, the moment brings contentment, satisfaction and profound happiness. How and where these qualities manifest will be made clear by the surrounding cards.

In health matters, vitality is restored and a physical peak is reached. Indeed, the inner peace it denotes can only improve health by banishing stress and sharpening the senses so that pleasure is gained from them. An appetite for all that life can offer is signalled here.

Emotionally, an intensely rewarding period may be expected. All kinds of close relationships flourish. If there have been difficulties, these

Reversed Meaning

The Nine of Cups reversed warns against arrogant complacency. There may well be an urge simply to sit back – to take things completely for granted and stop putting any effort into a creative project or relationship. Eventually, everything could be spoilt as a result.

A loving relationship may be stagnating. This card often turns up when a couple have stopped trying to surprise or delight one another. When linked to work issues, lack of effort or enthusiasm could undermine a successful project. Approach each day with positive intentions and you will not risk losing those things you truly value.

TEN OF CUPS

KEYWORDS

UPRIGHT: A full heart

REVERSED: A sense of loss

Symbolism of the Card

The Ten of Cups represents the zenith of an emotional cycle. Here, ten cups form a pyramid and the waters of love and creativity flow harmoniously down either side of it. The triangular arrangement of cups symbolizes a peak, which is one of the meanings linked with the number ten.

culmination of your efforts. And, while it is primarily a card of the heart, it should not be interpreted as a 'relationship' card unless other symbols support this meaning. The overflowing joys expressed here are essentially spiritual, and refer to the energy of love as a positive cosmic force which may, or may not, be channelled into a romantic union.

Upright Meaning

Traditionally, the Ten of Cups was said to mean 'perfection of the human heart'. The happiness associated with this card has a lasting quality, for it represents an outflowing of love between individuals. There are similarities with the Nine of Cups, for both symbolize joy. But the Ten of Cups speaks of permanence, and suggests a more outward and visible manifestation of love. Any personal links signified by this card will endure.

This card frequently acts as an affirmation of success, good fortune and all-round abundance. This is especially true when it appears at the end of a 'question and answer' spread, such as the Celtic Cross or Horseshoe – it promises a brilliant

Reversed Meaning

When reversed, this card signifies loss and disruption in the emotional realm. Relationships are the main focus but anything you are attached to may be subject to upheaval and change. A period of quarrelling or disagreement does not always mean permanent loss of love. As always, this card must be read in context.

Major changes of country or home are also signified when this card is reversed. When this meaning applies to you, you may experience sadness because you will miss old friends and neighbours – or even a home. A sense of dislocation and disruption is increased when the Tower appears nearby in the spread.

THE MINOR ARCANA

PAGE~PRINCESS OF CUPS

KEYWORDS

UPRIGHT: **Imagination • Gentleness**

REVERSED: **Bad dreams**

Symbolism of the Card

The Page~Princess of Cups is shown as an androgynous water spirit accompanied by two seahorses, denoting undersea journeys. Scallop shells underline the message of movement, linked to the Pages~Princesses. They are all symbols of regeneration, pilgrimage and birth – the goddess of love, Aphrodite, rose at birth from a scallop shell.

Upright Meaning

This card represents a messenger from the element of water, and from the world of creativity, love and dreams. When denoting a person, this Page is a dreamy child or young adolescent of either sex who may be psychic, artistic, a little vague and very sensitive. Such a child is often lost in a world of their own; indeed, they may create imaginary friends. Any difficulties this child may experience frequently involve imaginary terrors or fears and phobias.

Reversed Meaning

The Page of Cups reversed has swum into the waters of the unconscious. It signifies emotional confusion, spiritual delusions and an inability to communicate with clarity. It is as if everything is shrouded in mist, with all the edges blurred. This interpretation may refer to a personal mood, a prevailing atmosphere in a love or business situation, or it can describe someone's state of mind.

Abstract Meaning

As a messenger from the unknown, this card signifies creative, spiritual and loving feelings surfacing in your life. You may experience these as an increase in intuition, an active dream life, strong 'gut feelings' or a particular interest in paranormal and mysterious subjects. The presence of the Moon or the High Priestess often serves to confirm this meaning. When enquiring about love, this Page~Princess suggests you are ready to receive love because your heart is softening and beginning to open, like a flower in the sunshine. The Empress, Ace of Cups, Two of Cups or the Lovers amplify this interpretation. In a short spread, this card can represent happy news, usually from someone close.

KNIGHT OF CUPS

KEYWORDS
UPRIGHT: Romantic • Inspirational • Visionary
REVERSED: Loss of direction

Symbolism of the Card

This Knight is shown as a young merman. Seahorses have entwined their tails to form a heart. This heart signifies the wisdom of emotion, of valuing the qualities of compassion and unconditional love that radiate from an open heart. Pointed shells and fronds of seaweed evoke the Knight's underwater realm.

Upright Meaning

The Knight of Cups represents an archetypal young hero, the Grail Knight, whose story came to particular prominence during the medieval era of Courtly Love. Any individual signified by this card, therefore, carries the same visions and ideals somewhere within him. Sensitivity, artistic gifts, spiritual impulses and receptive characteristics represent his highest qualities.

As a symbol of the search for love, this card often signals the arrival of a special lover in your life. At this stage, love is exquisite and dreamlike – pure chemistry and romance. The challenges of this relationship are yet to come, for this is the dawning of a union that could become an enduring love.

As a messenger, the Knight of Cups brings up feelings of love and creativity. Such powerful impulses have a tendency to overflow into every part of your existence. This card tells you that you must follow the path of the heart now.

Reversed Meaning

When reversed, this card represents a withdrawal from active life, or denotes someone who cannot act on their dreams and feelings. This individual has talent and originality, but is afraid of failure and so stagnates. This position also means that a lover is leaving; to discover the circumstances and full implications of this, look at the surrounding cards.

Abstract Meaning

Developing intuition, artistic gifts and exploring your inner world are all suggested. Places where people learn creative skills or expand their spiritual side are often signified, too. If you are aware of a lack of direction, this card can indicate the most productive path for you to follow at this time in your life.

THE MINOR ARCANA

QUEEN OF CUPS

KEYWORDS

UPRIGHT: Self-contained • Feminine • Nurturing
REVERSED: Icy • Distant • Submerged

TRADITIONALLY, THIS CARD REPRESENTS A WOMAN WHO IS CONNECTED WITH LOVE, RELATIONSHIPS AND CREATIVITY.

Symbolism of the Card

The Queen of Cups is shown as a beautiful mermaid combing her hair, the outer symbol of her intensely feminine powers. She gazes into a bejewelled goblet, lost in secret dreams and perceiving visions of the future. Her scallop shells link her with Aphrodite, the goddess of love and pleasure, while her fishtail connects her to numerous fishtailed mother goddesses who predate the alluring sirens whom Ovid named 'the green daughters of the sea'. The dolphin with her was a mammal which in Roman, Greek and Christian myths guided the souls of the dead across the sea to the Isles of the Blest.

Upright Meaning

The Queen of Cups symbolizes the mother and siren combined. She is soft, feminine and fertile in mind, body and spirit. She is the epitome of femininity in its most nurturing form. And yet there is also something self-contained, secret and unattainable about her. As a human woman, the Queen of Cups is traditionally artistic, exceptionally psychic or spiritual, often musical, and is possessed of great taste and charisma. She is the sympathetic friend, the loving mother, the gentle and yielding beloved. She freely expresses her emotions, is often moved to tears and is capable of showing great empathy towards troubled souls. Her untouchable qualities can puzzle, mystify or even enrage others for, at some level, like the sea goddess that she is, she can never be fully possessed, known or controlled.

As a woman, the Queen of Cups may signify your mother or someone who plays that role in your life. She can appear as a healer, therapist, spiritual adviser, artistic or creative professional, or muse. She is any woman who exerts a fascinating or mysterious allure, who is loved by the querent, or who inspires dreams and visions.

Reversed Meaning

The Queen of Cups reversed is the spirit of icy waters, the deep, dark depths of the oceans where no human being can survive. She is the Snow Queen of fairytales, the impenetrable Ice Maiden, the dangerous siren who lures sailors to certain death in her elemental kingdom. As a human woman, she may have frozen emotions or talents – neither feeling nor creative achievement can flow in her life. Usually, this stems from some painful emotional wound that has not yet been resolved and healed. The traditional interpretation of this card reversed is a sorrowful woman. She may also be a woman who unsettles others through her manipulative behaviour, emotional dependency and an inability to experience happiness. She can drain others of their vital energies, for she is for ever empty and unfulfilled inside.

Abstract Meaning

As an abstract card, the Queen of Cups represents all endeavours where fantasy is made real. The cinema industry is a typical example. She also denotes professions or organizations dealing with emotions and sexuality, including relationship counselling, sex therapy, fertility clinics, drug rehabilitation centres and therapeutic techniques involving water.

THE MINOR ARCANA

KING OF CUPS

KEYWORDS

UPRIGHT: Magnetic • Instinctive • Emotional
REVERSED: Unfaithful • Destructive

TRADITIONALLY, THIS CARD REPRESENTS A MAN WHO IS CONNECTED WITH LOVE, RELATIONSHIPS AND CREATIVITY.

Symbolism of the Card

The King of Cups is shown as a water spirit, a sinuous fishtailed merman. He is accompanied by the king of the fishes, the dolphin – a mammal that was once believed to guide the souls of the dead to their rest. The King's trident, which he holds in his left hand, is a traditional symbol of the fertile powers of water. The pointed shells and seaweed also link him with the sea.

Upright Meaning

The charismatic King of Cups is a powerful and unusual man. His 'feminine' side is well-developed, expressing itself as intuition, creative talent, emotion and a deep sensitivity. Such traits are often well-concealed, for he is secretive and protects his inner world.

When representing a colleague or business contact, he denotes a creative thinker, someone who is not afraid to rely on their hunches or to take an unusual or even eccentric approach to problem-solving. He can often be found working in the media, the music business, speculative concerns (alongside the King of Wands), the arts and sometimes medicine or psychotherapy. In his working life he is often successful, for his maverick approach allows him to seize opportunities that a more cautious person would reject.

As a lover, this card symbolizes a passionate challenge. His intense feelings demand an equally emotional response from his partner. Flirtation for fun does not attract this man. When he flatters someone his interest has already been captured and, if encouraged, he will readily enter into a relationship. He is highly sexed, very sensual, and definitely not for the faint-hearted.

His sensitivity may be his downfall, for he can easily take offence and thus reject people or situations that benefit him. A vengeful enemy, he believes in the saying 'revenge is a dish best served cold'.

Reversed Meaning

At his most malefic, the King of Cups reversed represents a relentless enemy or a man who is destined to betray or seriously disappoint you. This interpretation will be affirmed by other cards – notably the Ten of Swords, Three of Swords and the Moon reversed.

This card can describe someone who is depressed or is behaving in a self-destructive manner. The King of Cups' creative energies have been turned against him, and he seeks to lose himself in a dream world – often with the aid of drugs, alcohol, excessive sleep, negative escapism or hermit-like withdrawal.

In a relationship reading, this King symbolizes the habitually unfaithful lover. His ability to deceive partners is matched by his ability to deceive himself, for he can easily imagine he is in love with two or more people at any one time. Finally, the King of Cups reversed stands for a confused partner who is unable to commit, yet unable to cut the ties that bind him to somebody. His ambivalence can be destructive to more straightforward types who, perversely, are attracted by his enigmatic ways.

Abstract Meaning

In a reading designed to clarify career questions, the King of Cups signifies spiritual and cultural endeavours. Specifically, these are music and the performing arts; the visual arts; publishing – especially illustrated books; galleries and museums. They may be spiritually inclined businesses such as alternative medical practices; therapy clinics; support groups; astrologers and psychics; and all centres offering personal-growth techniques and courses to the general public. Secret societies can be denoted also, particularly those that have ritualistic or religious interests.

Part Three

HOW TO USE THE RENAISSANCE TAROT

YOUR TAROT CARDS ARE LIKE A MAGICAL KEY THAT CAN UNLOCK THE DOORS OF PERCEPTION. THEY CAN MAKE VISIBLE THE LANDSCAPE OF DREAMS, THE TIMELESS, ELUSIVE DIMENSION THAT EXISTS SOMEWHERE ALONGSIDE OUR OWN. USED WISELY, THE SYMBOLIC LANGUAGE OF THE TAROT CAN HELP YOU TO INCREASE YOUR AWARENESS, TAKE PRACTICAL DECISIONS AND ASSESS SITUATIONSFOR YOURSELF AND OTHERS.

Tarot Reading – A Basic Guide

When you use your tarot cards you may come to realize their ultimate paradox – that both fate and self-determination seem to coexist side by side, and we can never be sure which one is creating the intricate patterns of life. Perhaps this is why the ancient Greeks pictured the Fates as three implacable goddesses – Clotho, Lachesis and Atropos. Clotho spun the thread of life on her spindle, Lachesis measured it with her rod and Atropos cut it with her shears. Neither human beings nor powerful deities could influence these figures for good or ill.

We can control our choices, our attitudes, and decide whether or not we will embrace life wholeheartedly – and these things consequently affect our experiences. And yet, from time to time, a larger, more mysterious pattern is glimpsed. With time and experience, the tarot may show you a little of both.

Getting to Know the Renaissance Tarot

Successful tarot reading begins when you are familiar with your cards. There are various ways to achieve this, and it is helpful to try them all until you find a way (or ways) that suits you. These are not rules, merely suggestions. You can:
• Play with the deck, picking out any cards that especially appeal to you. Using a special notebook, write down your impressions. Some images may delight you, others alarm or disturb you. Do you know why? How might these reactions affect your interpretation of a spread? Keep going until you have worked through the whole of the Major Arcana. You might also like

to try this with the court cards and Aces of the Minor Arcana.

- Place a card on your bedside table or under your pillow before you go to sleep. Look at it intently before drifting off to sleep. Ask your subconscious to send you inspiration about the card in a dream. When you awake, write down your impressions. Did you dream? Did you feel any connection with the symbol on the card? Write down your thoughts or feelings in a dream journal.
- Pick any card that appeals to you and weave a story around it. A small spread – such as the Horseshoe – can also be used to do this. Don't be concerned about accurate meanings; the keywords on each page are enough to act as prompts. The idea is to develop your intuition and your feeling for the cards as mythic symbols.
- Practise laying out the cards, using the spreads in this book, or any others that appeal to you. Simply look up the meanings of the cards, one by one, and write brief notes detailing the spread and which card fell where. You can do spreads for world events, political situations, absent friends or yourself. Remember, you are developing your skills. Do not take the results too seriously, or become obsessed with laying the cards out for yourself. They will cease to give you an accurate picture if you often use them for personal reassurance.

Choosing a Significator

Once you have prepared for a tarot reading by relaxing, clearing a special space and emptying your mind of mental 'chatter', you need to select an appropriate spread (*see pages 178–85*). If you are dealing with a complex situation, or a time of many changes, you will probably need to use several spreads – one that offers a general picture, such as the Romany spread, and one that can answer specific questions, such as the Horseshoe. It is helpful to decide which spreads you will be using before you begin.

Some spreads ask you to choose a significator. This is the name given to a court card (either the

Sun	Element	Significator
Aries, Leo, Sagittarius	Fire	King or Queen of Wands
Taurus, Virgo, Capricorn	Earth	King or Queen of Pentacles
Gemini, Aquarius, Libra	Air	King or Queen of Swords
Cancer, Scorpio, Pisces	Water	King or Queen of Cups

King or Queen) that you choose to represent yourself, or the subject of your reading when you are looking at the cards for another person. One of the simplest ways to select a significator is to base it upon the individual's birth sign element – fire, earth, air or water (*see chart on page 173*).

Another way of deciding which card to use is to assess someone's personality type and, using the descriptions in this book, to make your decision – is he or she predominantly a thinker, a practical type, a creative spirit or an intuitive extrovert? Lastly, you may simply use your intuition, or you may prefer to ask your enquirer to pick a card that appeals to them.

The next step is to shuffle the deck thoroughly. The person for whom the reading is being done should shuffle, either in the normal way or by 'washing' the cards. To do this, place the deck face down on the table and move the cards around in a circular motion, spreading them out and finally gathering them up again to reform the deck. If the first method is chosen, make sure you turn some of the cards upside down before replacing them in the deck so that you get some reversed cards. These may, or may not, appear in the subsequent spread. Either way, that will have a bearing on the reading.

Once you or your enquirer has put the cards back into a neat pile, the deck should be cut with the left hand into three piles of any size. Rebuild the deck by arranging the piles in a different order – the middle one underneath or on top, the final pile as the first section, and so on. Do whatever you feel like doing; using your intuition is always more important than following some arcane ritual. Now you are ready to deal out the cards from the top of your new deck, following the layout of the spread you have chosen.

The positions of the cards will help you to interpret them correctly, as each position has a name and meaning which offers you a context. For instance, the Horoscope Spread follows the traditional design of a zodiac birth chart – each position relates to a different area of life. So, if the Hierophant appears in position one of this spread, it might describe someone who is fairly conventional. In position nine, however, it would suggest further education, because this position is associated with exploring new frontiers through study or travel. The context of your cards is very important, and helps to eliminate confusion and strengthens your interpretative abilities.

Each of the Minor Arcana's court cards has an extra category, which describes its abstract meaning. This relates to their impersonal meanings – when they symbolize a place, business or any other subject area that is not directly related to feelings, thoughts and individuals. Using the abstract meanings of the

Minor Arcana is often suggested by the position of the card in a spread – to continue with the previous example, a court card might describe an individual if it appeared in the first or seventh position of the Horoscope Spread, but an abstract meaning would be more appropriate for a position such as the tenth, relating to career, or the sixth, relating to health and everyday working life. Ultimately, there are no hard-and-fast rules; only that potent mix of common sense and intuitive wisdom which guides all successful divination.

Finally, never read the cards when you, or your enquirer, feel distracted, emotionally upset, physically unwell or angry. The best results are obtained when you are in a relaxed state of mind and are not overly anxious about the answers to your questions. Anxiety and mental strain block both individual intuition and spiritual guidance. 'Leap, and the net will appear' might be a good motto to adopt when trying to unravel the secrets of past, present and future ...

Reading with Confidence

Learning to read the cards can seem daunting at first. But as you begin to trust your developing intuition, and become familiar with the cards, your interpretations will feel more and more natural. Preparing yourself for a reading is a crucial part of this process; your rituals will tell your subconscious what you are about to do, and help you to get into the right mood. There are many traditional rituals associated with tarot reading, so simply select what appeals to you personally – or invent your own. Preparation and intent are more important than rules. You can:

- Keep your deck wrapped up in a special cloth – silk or velvet bring a feeling of sensuality and symbolize riches and special occasions.
- Have a special cloth that you can spread out on the table where you read the cards. This cloth is used only for this purpose, and kept immaculate. Again, velvet and silk are traditional.
- Use incense, natural room sprays, aromatic oils or light-bulb ring-burners to scent the atmosphere before and during a reading. Citrus scents sharpen the mind; gums and resins, such as frankincense, create a spiritual atmosphere; flower scents are often soothing.
- Light a candle, or candles, in the room where you are working. White symbolizes purity; silver vibrates with the spirit realms; blue is the colour of meditation; pink stands for spiritual love. You may like to research other colour correspondences and choose whatever attracts you most.
- Play some calming music before you begin. Classical music, music from ancient cultures – pick something that takes you outside the mundane world and helps you to tune in to your intuitive voice.

- Take a few moments to close your eyes, relax, breathe slowly and deeply, and ask for guidance from your higher self, subconscious mind, guides, angels or whatever feels right to you.
- Choose all, or some, of these rituals to help you. Remember, they are the tools you can use to create atmosphere and promote intuition.
- Never let anyone play with your cards in a casual way. Store them somewhere safe, respect them and take care of them.
- Select the right spread for your purpose, and always pay close attention to the meaning of a card's position. This will allow you to refine your interpretation.
- View a spread like a painting. What does the overall picture suggest? Are there a lot of Major Arcana cards? Does one Minor suit dominate? What kind of images catch your attention? How do you feel when looking at the spread?
- Let the spirit of fun and laughter prevail. Creativity, intuition and play are linked – don't take yourself, or your prognostications, too seriously. And never use the cards to pass judgement or gain power.

Timing

Sooner or later in a tarot reading, the question 'when?' is asked. Most professional tarot readers will readily admit that attempting to time events with the cards is difficult, elusive and often inaccurate. After many years' experience reading the tarot, I have concluded that there are several reasons for this.

In our everyday lives we are used to clocks and calendars, which neatly parcel up our days, months and years. So we think of time, when we think of it at all, as something supremely logical that we can measure and define. But there are many ways of measuring time, and a dazzling array of measurements to choose from – ask any scientist. Our perception of time is another elastic concept – our dreams seem to last for hours, although they may flicker past our internal screen in only a few minutes or seconds by a conventional clock. And who has not experienced time flying by when they are absorbed by creativity or love, or felt every second last for ever when waiting impatiently for important news? The inner calendar also seems to operate at different speeds, at various times in life. What is intended to be a six-month reading, for example, may cover three months for one person, or as long as two years for another.

I have observed that people seem to live their lives at varying speeds; there are times when either everything is in slow motion or it passes by at dizzying speed. As a general guideline, the presence of the Hanged Man, the Moon, the Hermit, or a large number of reversed

TIMING

cards, suggests worldly events unfolding at a slow pace, for the focus is very much on spiritual concerns, inner development and personal unfoldment. The Wheel of Fortune or a majority of Wands (upright) usually indicates speed and energy – outer events tumble over one another, new people, new directions; at such times the inner world is no longer absorbing energy for its own purposes.

Bearing all this in mind, there are two simple methods you can try. The first method uses the Twos, Threes and Fours of the Minor Arcana suits. Each card represents a particular month, as shown in the table at the bottom of this page.

Shuffle the whole deck, meditating upon your question. Cut the deck into three piles, reassemble in a new order, and begin turning up the cards from the top of the deck. Count off thirteen cards, only stopping if one of the cards indicated above turns up. This will be your answer. For instance, Two of Wands refers to June. If none appear, begin to count off another thirteen cards. If a card of the month has still not appeared, you can try for a third time, but you should be prepared for a delay, and the answer may not be reliable. The resolution to your question is elusive, undecided or very unlikely to happen at all.

The second method only uses the Minor Arcana. Shuffle the cards, cut and reassemble the deck as usual. Deal off the top of the deck – counting up to thirteen cards if necessary – until you reach one of the four Aces. If it is upright, the answer is 'yes'; if reversed, 'no'. If no Ace appears in the first pile, count off a second and, if necessary, a third. No Aces in any of the piles means that hidden factors are influencing the outcome and a definite answer is not possible yet. Using the seasonal correspondences you can determine exactly when you will get your wish. So, for instance, an upright Ace of Pentacles would mean that your question will be happily resolved in the winter, while a reversed Ace of Wands suggests that you will be disappointed in the summer.

Season/Suit	Two	Three	Four
Spring/Swords	March	April	May
Summer/Wands	June	July	August
Autumn/Cups	September	October	November
Winter/Pentacles	December	January	February

HOW TO USE THE RENAISSANCE TAROT

TRADITIONAL LAYOUTS

The Horseshoe Spread

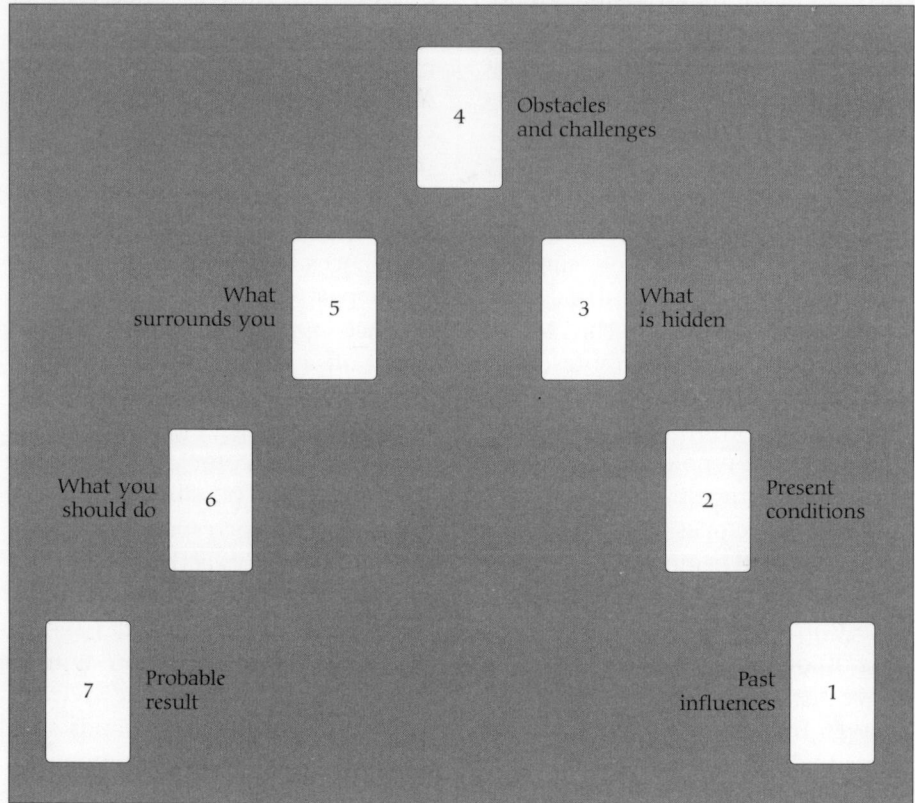

Shaped like a crescent moon, this popular spread is found in a number of versions, using five, six, seven or even sixteen cards. Here we use seven cards, a mystical number that is in tune with the spread's lunar vibrations.

The Horseshoe Spread is useful when you want a straightforward answer to a direct question, such as 'Should I apply for this job?' For a broader picture of events and influences, use the Romany or the Horoscope Spreads. In this spread, each position has a very specific sphere of influence and meaning that offers you a precise context in which to interpret it. Great clarity is needed to get the best out of this spread – it may help if you write

TRADITIONAL LAYOUTS

down your question first. You will find that some situations are so complex that they need several questions in order to explore all the options. Frame your question so that a 'yes' or 'no' answer can be given each time.

Shuffle the deck thoroughly, using this process as a time in which to concentrate upon your (or your enquirer's) question. The person who needs an answer always shuffles the deck. Shuffle for as long as you need to, and then cut the deck into three piles, face down. Reassemble the deck, placing the last pile cut on top of the first pile, and placing the second on top of that. Deal seven cards from the top, placing them face up in the positions shown on the diagram on the facing page. Alternatively, you may like to shuffle the deck, fan it out, face down, on the table, and invite the enquirer to pick seven cards from anywhere that feels right. Again, place each card, face up, in position as it is selected.

CARD 1 *Past influences.*
How influential is this card? Is it from the Major Arcana or the Minor Arcana? Is it upright or reversed? The past may have everything to do with present circumstances or, alternatively, may wield very little influence.

CARD 2 *Present conditions.*
This card may be subjective, and relate to thoughts and feelings, or objective, and relate to tangible, known circumstances or people.

CARD 3 *What is hidden.*
Unforeseen circumstances, secrets, situations that have not been taken into account – all these factors can influence the outcome of the subject of the reading.

CARD 4 *Obstacles and challenges.*
These may be major disruptions, or they may represent passing conditions. Again, as with card 2, check to see whether this card suggests thoughts (often denoted by the suit of Swords), feelings (signified by the suit of Cups) or larger, more worldly events, suggested by Major Arcana cards or the suits of Wands and Pentacles.

CARD 5 *What surrounds you.*
This position describes the current background to your question, the environment, and the presence of others (where appropriate). Help, guidance or other people's attitudes – positive or negative – towards this question may all be revealed here.

CARD 6 *What you should do.*
Suggestions for action, biding your time, enlisting practical help or other means will be signified here.

CARD 7 *Probable result.*
This card assumes that you will take the action suggested by card 6, and overcome any of the challenges revealed by cards 3 and 4.

The Romany Spread

COLUMN ONE	COLUMN TWO	COLUMN THREE	COLUMN FOUR	COLUMN FIVE	COLUMN SIX	COLUMN SEVEN
1	4	7	10	13	16	19
2	5	8	11	14	17	20
3	6	9	12	15	18	21

The classic Romany Spread uses twenty-one cards, which may be laid out in vertical columns of three cards each, or three horizontal rows of seven cards (*see the diagram above*). This layout is believed to have originated with the Romany gypsies, whose fabled psychic gifts and fortune-telling skills spring from their Indian origins. Gypsies regarded the tarot as a book of knowledge and wisdom which could be read by anyone who understood its mysterious, deeply symbolic language.

The Romany Spread reveals both present and future influences, potential and hidden factors. The enquirer shuffles the cards and cuts the deck into three piles, placing them face down on the table. The reader then reassembles the deck, placing the last pile on top of the first one, and placing the middle pile on top or underneath, as he or she wishes. The cards are then dealt off the top of the deck as follows:

COLUMN ONE *Self.*
(Cards 1, 2 and 3)
Reveals what most concerns the enquirer at this time, and also suggests what is awakening within – whether creative energy, confusion, ambition, and so on. Nascent potential or influences are often symbolized by the third card, at the bottom of the column.

COLUMN TWO *The environment.*
(Cards 4, 5 and 6)
Close relationships of every kind – lover, family, friends, colleagues, for example – are described in this

column. Sometimes it describes events that are happening to someone close, sometimes the general atmosphere surrounding the enquirer at home, socially or at work.

COLUMN THREE *Hopes, fears, dreams, wishes.*
(Cards 7, 8 and 9)
How does this column relate to the first column? What is the prevailing feeling of this column? What is the enquirer aiming at? Are there any obstacles to progress? Or do the cards suggest the achievement of dreams and fulfilment of hopes?

COLUMN FOUR *What you expect.*
(Cards 10, 11 and 12)
Plans in progress, projects in motion, known factors. Progress, success, delays or disappointments may all be revealed here.

COLUMN FIVE *Hidden destiny.*
(Cards 13, 14 and 15)
Here are the surprises, unforeseen developments and hidden influences at work. Traditionally, this is the column where karma, destiny or fate is glimpsed.

COLUMN SIX *Near future.*
(Cards 16, 17 and 18)
What may happen to the enquirer in the next two months or so.

COLUMN SEVEN *Further future.*
(Cards 19, 20 and 21)
Events taking place from four to six months ahead are indicated here.

Columns 4, 5 and 6 may tie in with this one, so that together they tell an unfolding story. Alternatively, this column may seem to be unrelated to the rest of the spread, perhaps as a result of the hidden factors described in column 5. When this happens, a twist of fate may be in store for the enquirer.

Variation on the Romany Spread – Past, Present, Future

When using this spread, you should pick a significator before you begin to shuffle the cards. Replace the card in the deck before shuffling and cutting the cards as usual, and then dealing twenty-one cards off the top of the deck. Lay out the cards in three horizontal rows of seven cards each. The first row (cards 1 to 7) represents the past, the middle row (cards 8 to 14) shows the current circumstances, and the last row (cards 15 to 21) foretells the probable future. Where does the card representing the enquirer fall? If in the first row, they are influenced by past events, perhaps to an unhelpful degree. If in the middle row, they may give little thought to tomorrow, or be happily aware of the present moment. If in the last row, they may be extremely focused on their plans, or be living in a dream – unable to enjoy or accept reality. The surrounding cards will embroider and enlarge upon these meanings. When no significator appears in the spread, the enquirer is being objective, detached and balanced.

HOW TO USE THE RENAISSANCE TAROT

The Horoscope Spread

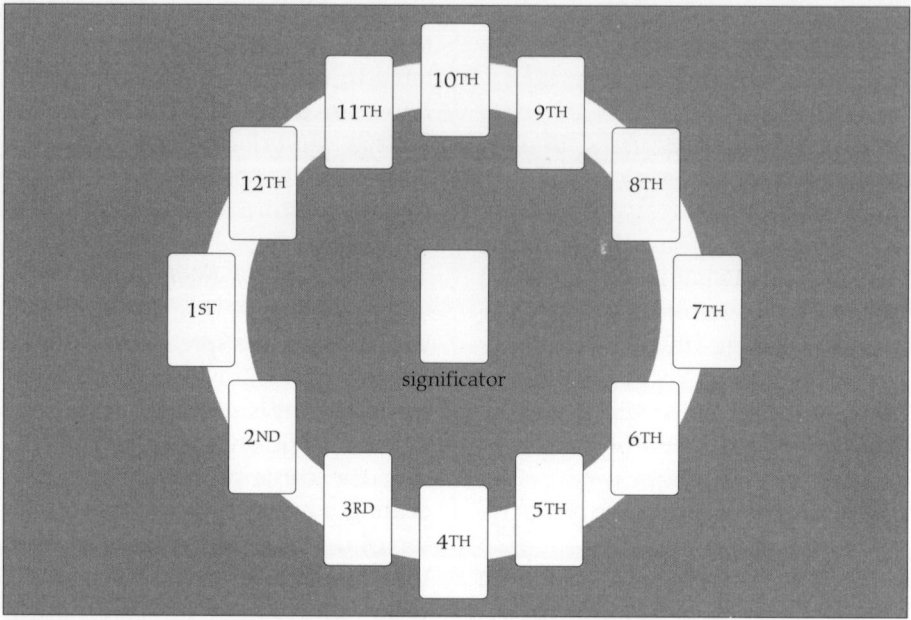

The Horoscope Spread is based on the traditional houses of the horoscope or birth chart. It will appeal to astrologers but is also suitable for anyone who would like to gain an overall view of their character, circumstances and potential. Each of the twelve houses rules a specific area of life. Cards in each house must be read in this context. Choose a significator to represent the subject of the reading before you begin, and place it in the centre of the circle. Alternatively, choose the significator and replace it in the deck before cutting and dealing the cards. The house it appears in will be most significant. When it fails to appear, you or the enquirer are detached from your current life circumstances.

When you are more experienced, you can shuffle again and add one more card to each 'house'. You can repeat this process once more so you will then have three cards in each position – but do not try this out until you are very familiar with the deck. The houses are as follows:

1ST HOUSE *The self, personality and self-expression. Image.*
If you have chosen a central significator, read this card in combination with it. How do the two cards relate? If this card is from the Minor Arcana how does its suit connect with the significator? Check the resonance

and dissonance rules in the introductions to each suit to find out.

2ND HOUSE *What you value.*
Finances and possessions.

3RD HOUSE *Communications, short trips, brothers and sisters, news.*

4TH HOUSE *Your home as emotional refuge, roots, childhood, mother.*
Traditionally, the home of the soul.

5TH HOUSE *Creativity, gambling, pleasures, love affairs.*
Check the seventh house for possible partners, the tenth house for creative outlets. Many creative cards also denote romantic involvement. Check the eighth house for indications of infatuation, obsession, intense love affairs.

6TH HOUSE *Routine, health and hygiene, pets, service to others.*

7TH HOUSE *Partnerships, whether business or marital.*
Also the house of open enemies and competitors.

8TH HOUSE *Transformation through others' resources.*
Money, for example. Transformative experiences through love, spiritual inspiration, encounters with the unknown in any sphere or form.

9TH HOUSE *Far horizons and unfamiliar experiences.*
Long-distance travel, mental studies and exploration, philosophical study or metaphysical adventure. Unfamiliar experiences, foreign cultures and people, expansive events.

10TH HOUSE *Direction, career, goals, aspirations.*
Also, the father, when appropriate.

11TH HOUSE *Friends, social groups, societies and professional bodies.*
The social structure of life. Love received from others.

12TH HOUSE *The unconscious mind.*
Psychic events, confinement, what is hidden or imprisoned inside or in the world. The house of hidden enemies, experienced either as inner impulses or as outer events and people. Karma and destiny.

Connecting the houses through themes, as explained below, can amplify your interpretation. Read the three cards connected with the houses together, after first interpreting them separately, so as to gain an overview of the area in question. The following suggestions are based on astrology and may help you to see the larger pattern revealed by this spread:

PERSONAL LIFE *Houses 1, 5, 9.*

WORK AND FINANCES *Houses 2, 6, 10.*

OTHER PEOPLE *Houses 3, 7, 11.*

SECRET FOUNDATIONS *Houses 4, 8, 12.*

HOW TO USE THE RENAISSANCE TAROT

The Celtic Cross

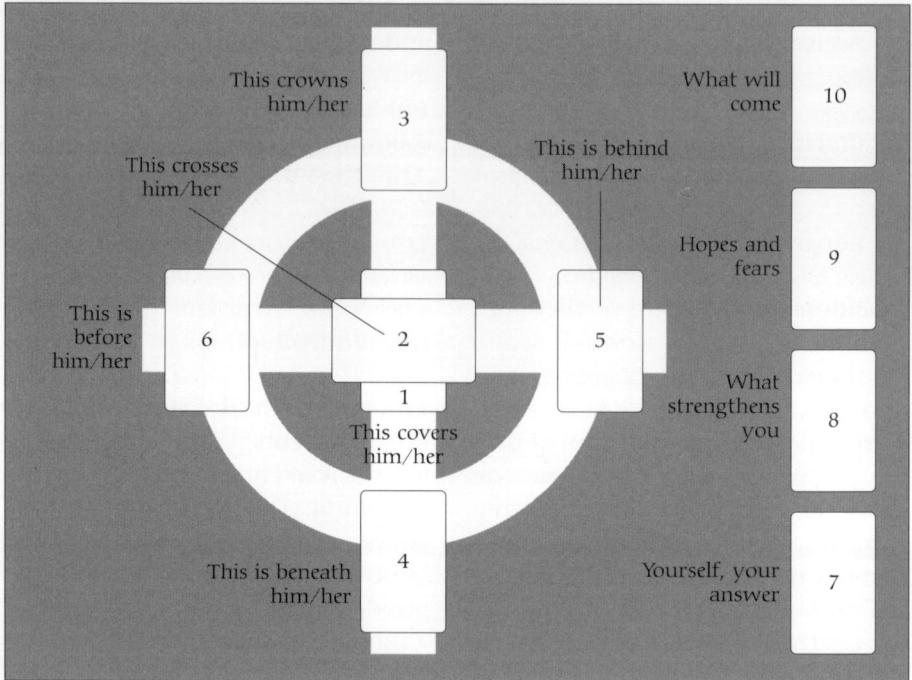

The Celtic Cross is generally thought to date from the seventeenth century, which makes it one of the oldest tarot spreads in existence. It was a favourite of Arthur Edward Waite, influential occultist and the creator of the famous Rider Waite tarot deck at the beginning of the twentieth century.

Although it only employs ten cards, plus a significator, this spread is designed to be read in depth with great sensitivity and awareness. It is suitable for a single question or a concentrated analysis of a situation – such as career direction, love life, and so on. You may use this spread with the Major Arcana alone or with the full deck of seventy-eight cards. When selecting the Major Arcana, you will receive a very spiritual, powerful spread. Both enquirer and tarot reader should approach this with respect and a willingness to explore the compelling archetypes that these cards represent because they will offer much food for thought, meditation and intuitive analysis. Using the full deck will give you a broad picture.

Select your significator and place it on the table. (You can select this card from the Minor Arcana even when you plan to use the Major

Arcana for the rest of the layout.) Shuffle and cut the cards, dealing from the top of the deck and following the diagram on the facing page. Cards 7 to 10 may be laid face down and turned up once you have read cards 1 to 6. Be careful not to reverse them (either way) when you do this. The traditional name of each position is given here; some readers like to say the name of the position out loud as they place each card – but this is a personal choice. The cards are interpreted as follows:

CARD 1 *This covers him/her.*
It reveals the present circumstances, the problem – if any – and the current atmosphere in relation to the question posed by the enquirer.

CARD 2 *This crosses him/her.*
Whatever blocks or opposes the enquirer; which conflicts or challenges must be faced. This should be read in conjunction with card l.

CARD 3 *This crowns him/her.*
Developments in the near future, outcome, goals and progress.

CARD 4 *This is beneath him/her.*
Past influences, whether known or unknown, which have contributed to the present circumstances.

CARD 5 *This is behind him/her.*
Events, people or attitudes that are passing away and leaving the enquirer's life, thoughts or their current circumstances.

CARD 6 *This is before him/her.*
This card reveals the future events, forthcoming events, influences or people that may help or hinder the enquirer in their quest.

CARD 7 *Yourself, your answer.*
This card shows how the enquirer uses their abilities, talents, skills, mental attitude and so on, and how these may all affect the ultimate outcome in their life.

CARD 8 *What strengthens you.*
This card shows what is favourable in the enquirer's immediate environment, what and who is available to provide help for the enquirer, positive attributes and prevailing influences in general.

CARD 9 *Hopes and fears.*
The enquirer's own hopes and fears, inner dreams, secret wishes and expectations.

CARD 10 *What will come.*
The outcome, eventual result and whether or not it will be beneficial to the enquirer. Sometimes a court card appears here when you are using the whole deck. If its abstract meanings appear to be confusing or inappropriate to the rest of the reading, take this card as the significator for another Celtic Cross spread. This second spread will reveal how the person represented by the court card may affect the future, or which role they are destined to play in the enquirer's life.

HOW TO USE THE RENAISSANCE TAROT

Sample Readings

THESE TWO SAMPLE READINGS HAVE BEEN INCLUDED TO GIVE YOU AN IDEA OF HOW A TAROT SPREAD IS INTERPRETED IN PRACTICE.

Sample Spread One
A Career Reading for Delia

The first reading was for Delia, an artist and interior designer in her early thirties. She had reached a crossroads in her career, and needed to know whether she should continue to be employed by a company or to branch out on her own. The Celtic Cross was selected, since, although the question was simple, a number of factors were involved in Delia's decision.

CARD 1 The Tower reveals the need for dramatic change that our enquirer is experiencing. These feelings have been gathering strength for a long while and are about to erupt into consciousness. Delia's decision to have a reading indicates her intuitive awareness of this.

CARD 2 The Knight of Pentacles forms a favourable 'crossing' card, suggesting ambition and the ability to work hard to achieve it. In this

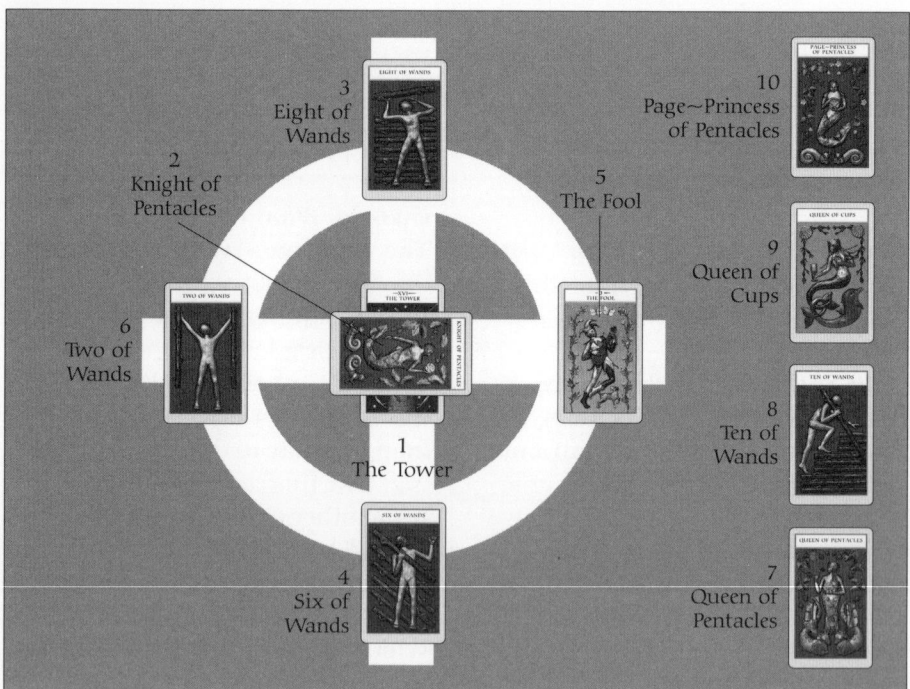

position it represents obstacles, and here they seem to relate to Delia's ability to believe in her own talents.

CARD 3 The Eight of Wands is the 'crowning' card of the spread, suggesting movement and news in the very near future.

CARD 4 The Six of Wands relates to the past. It affirms the message of the Knight of Pentacles by suggesting that Delia has come a lot further than she may realize.

CARD 5 The Fool describes factors that are passing away now. Delia's early career moves are behind her, she is already established and has proved her talents in the real world.

CARD 6 The Two of Wands suggests successful deals and introduces the idea of a working partnership in the near future. Combined with the Eight of Wands, this reveals an option that Delia has not yet considered. Setting up on her own with a partner may solve her dilemma.

CARD 7 The Queen of Pentacles describes Delia's state of mind and her feelings concerning her question. It shows that practical issues, financial security and establishing a solid future are all important to her.

CARD 8 The Ten of Wands brings yet more fiery, creative energy into the spread – most appropriate for an interior designer, since Wands are connected with property matters, too. Great energy is directed into the career when this card appears. In this position, the card describes how others see Delia. Any potential business partner would be drawn to her ambition and energy.

CARD 9 The Queen of Cups falls in the position of hopes and expectations. It is read in combination with card 3, here the Eight of Wands. The Queen of Cups denotes imagination, fantasy and creativity. She may also signify Delia's new partner – further underlining the need to share the burdens of a business with a kindred spirit. This position often reveals deep needs and feelings – here, it seems that a business partner is the answer to Delia's dilemma.

CARD 10 The Page~Princess of Pentacles ends the spread on a practical note. Minor financial improvements can be expected, and rethinking the practical issues surrounding the question will pay dividends. Delia is on the verge of changes but all the ingredients are not yet in place. Once she acknowledges the need for a business associate, and works towards finding one, she will be able to expand and develop successfully in a new direction. Some tarot readers recommend dealing out a second spread when a court card appears in the tenth position. However, the Pages are often abstract in meaning, and here a second spread would seem to be unnecessary.

Sample Spread Two
A Question of Love

This spread was carried out at the end of a longer reading, to clarify matters for Jenny. Her previous relationship had ended and she had recently met a man she was very attracted to, and wondered if a relationship might develop between them. The Horseshoe Spread was used to place her question in a precise context, and to see what advice might be appropriate for her.

CARD 1 Here, the King of Wands represents Jenny's past, and refers to her previous partner. He is a fire sign man who was working abroad at the time of the tarot reading.

CARD 2 Here, the King of Pentacles represents the present, indicating Jenny's new love interest who, although not the earth sign which this card can suggest, is serious, sensual and ambitious – personal qualities suggested by this card.

CARD 3 The Sun indicates hidden factors, and exerts a joyful influence on the spread as a whole. It is also associated with hot countries, and suggests that Jenny may not have heard the last of her ex-boyfriend.

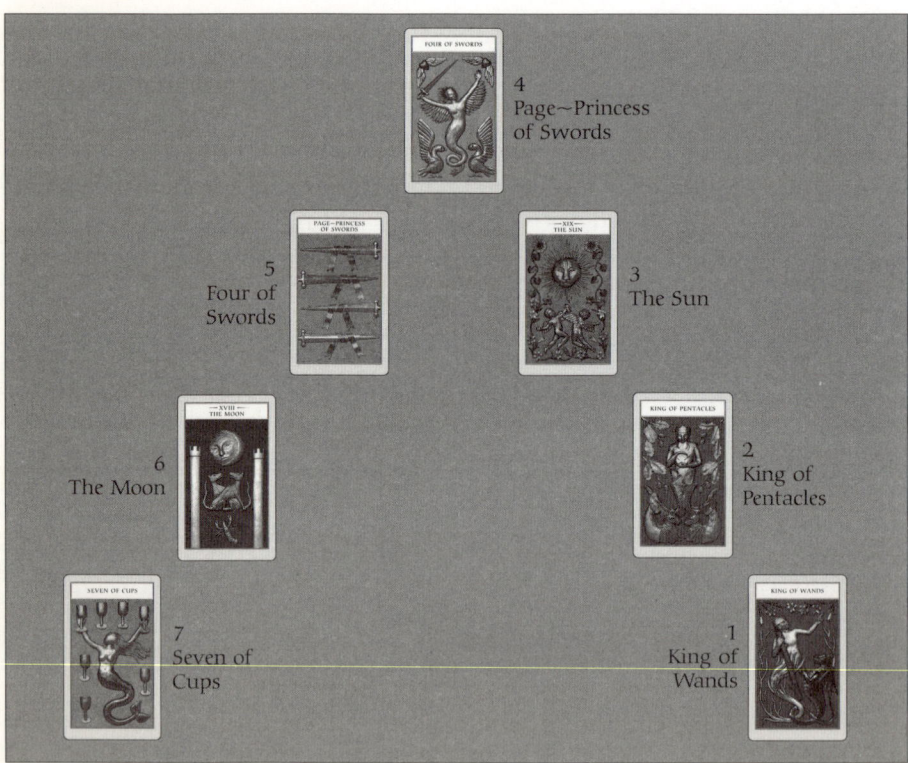

4 Page~Princess of Swords

5 Four of Swords

3 The Sun

6 The Moon

2 King of Pentacles

7 Seven of Cups

1 King of Wands

SAMPLE READINGS

CARD 4 In this position, the Page~Princess of Swords represents blocks or obstacles to the relationship. Gossip, perhaps about Jenny's previous relationship, might undermine her progress with her new friend. There could also be news that might influence the situation.

CARD 5 The Four of Swords depicts the environment surrounding the question. At the moment it would seem that everything is on hold, for this is a card of rest and recuperation rather than direct action.

CARD 6 The Moon offers advice. Here, it suggests that all is not as it appears, and that fantasies and dreams are casting a subtle spell. Jenny is advised to contact her own intuition, something she has already set in motion by consulting the cards. She may need a quiet time to discover how she feels about the past and the future before she can proceed in any direction.

CARD 7 In this position, the Seven of Cups describes the outcome if the advice of card 6 is taken. Here, it reveals romantic confusion and perhaps an overabundance of potential partners. The reading does not rule out her new love interest, since he appears firmly in the present, but the appearance of her former partner suggests that there may be unfinished business with him, and that she is not really as free as she appears or would like to be.

INTERPRETING A READING

These two sample readings have been included to show you how individual cards combine to create a forecast, or overview, of someone's situation. Only experience and familiarity with the cards can help you to achieve fluid interpretations, although you can certainly obtain accurate readings by using a book, such as this one. Intuition plays a crucial role, too. This will develop through allowing your eye to wander over the images, relaxing and seeing what they suggest to you.

Tarot reading is predominantly a right-brain activity – like art, music or meditation. And there is nothing the right brain likes better than play. Approach your readings with good sense and humour. Never use the cards to impose your own morality, judgement or world view on another person. In other words, do not play God. Any advice you do offer should take the form of encouraging someone to live out their dreams, or be strictly practical – for example, massage or exercise for someone feeling tense. It is also advisable to discourage dependency – on you, as a reader, or the cards. In this way you can avoid the murky waters of control, spiritual superiority and emotional manipulation. A reading is only a spiritual weather report – and it is up to the enquirer how he or she chooses to deal with the prevailing cosmic climate.

Finally, always take something in exchange for a reading. This might be something as simple as a bunch of flowers or a bar of chocolate, but an exchange is important both psychologically and spiritually. Enjoy yourself.

SYMBOLS

The symbols used in *The Renaissance Tarot* were inspired by existing tarot designs, alchemical art, Renaissance art, design and architectural detail, and by visual metaphors associated with myth and magic. Symbols, by their very nature, ultimately defy analysis or categorization because they speak to the non-rational part of our minds. The use of visual metaphors was particularly widespread during the Renaissance – artists plundered classical and oriental sources for inspiration, producing a rich brew of their own. The following list highlights some of the most common symbols that appear in *The Renaissance Tarot*.

FLOWERS Flowers, particularly roses, are used in many of the Major Arcana designs. They represent the feminine principle, spiritual beauty and the forces of life and death. Flowers have been linked with funerals and with the concept of eternal life for thousands of years.

ROSES In alchemical symbolism, roses denote the process of alchemy, sometimes called the rosarium. Roses are linked with myriad branches of mysticism, symbolizing both purity and passion, love and death, secrecy and unity.

INFINITY SYMBOL A figure-of-eight lying on its side is the mathematical symbol of infinity, and is also a mystical symbol of the endless flow of energy – of both active and receptive forces – which constitutes life itself.

CADUCEUS The caduceus, with its twin serpents intertwined up a stave, is a familiar symbol still used today by the medical profession. It is sometimes called the Staff of Asclepius, after the ancient god of healing. In alchemy it symbolizes the blending of fire and water, or active and receptive forces.

SERPENT As a snake with its tail in its mouth, the serpent represents the Ouroboros, or World Snake, the eternal cycles of life and death, and the hidden powers of nature. This symbol is found in diverse cultures all over the world. Snakes in general are associated with goddesses, symbolizing life and death, instinct, energy and renewal.

PILLARS Strength and stability were the traditional attributes of the pillars in King Solomon's temple. Pillars are also associated with gateways and thresholds of every kind because they represent the entrance to unknown or spiritual domains. Pillars are linked in symbolism with trees – for their strength – and with all forms of doors and gates.

MOON An ancient symbol of time, the Moon's phases are associated in numerous cultures with the continuous forces of growth, decay, culmination and renewal. The alchemical figure of Luna (Latin for 'Moon') represents silver, feminine powers and purity of the heart.

SUN An ancient symbol of both life and death, and our measure of the day's hours, the Sun denotes radiance and power, creativity, masculine forces and joy. It is associated with symbols such as the lion, eagle, ram, angels and white horses. The alchemical king, Sol (Latin for 'Sun'), represents gold, masculine forces and the intellect. The Sun is also a symbol of divine illumination.

VINE A life symbol, the vine and its grapes signify fertility, knowledge and sometimes they represent the Tree of Life itself. Greek myth links the vine with Dionysus, god of the vine, and Apollo, god of the reasoning intellect. Christian symbolism uses the vine as a metaphor for spiritual growth and faith.

Bibliography and Further Reading

Cavendish, Richard, *The Tarot*. London: Chancellor Press, 1988.
Cherry, John (editor), *Mythical Beasts*. London: British Museum Press, 1995.
Cooper, J. C., *Symbolic and Mythological Animals*. London: Aquarian/Thorsons, 1992.
von Franz, Marie-Louise, *Alchemy: An Introduction*. Toronto: Inner City Books, 1980.
Rachleff, Owen S., *The Occult in Art*. London: Cromwell Editions, 1990.
Roob, Alexander, *Alchemy and Mysticism*. Cologne: Taschen, 1997.
Tarnas, Richard, *The Passion of the Western Mind*. London: Pimlico, 1996.

About the Author

JANE LYLE is a writer on psychology, sex, sociology, paranormal and divination topics. She has built upon a childhood interest with in-depth research, studying and teaching tarot for over fifteen years. Previous titles include, among others, *The Lovers' Tarot*, *The Fortune Teller's Deck*, *Secrets of the Zodiac* and *The Key to the Tarot*. In addition, she has contributed to various volumes, including *The Macmillan Dictionary of the Paranormal* and *Natural Magic*. Jane also writes regularly for periodicals and newspapers in the UK.

About the Artist

HELEN JONES has been working as an illustrator since graduating from St Martin's School of Art in 1986. Her distinctive three-dimensional style is published in magazines and newspapers across Europe and in the US, as well as finding diverse applications from CD covers to murals for shop interiors. She exhibits her work widely and has won illustration awards in both the UK and the US.

Acknowledgements

Author's Acknowledgements

I would like to thank the following people for helping me manifest a long-cherished dream: to the team at Eddison Sadd Editions – Ian Jackson, Nick Eddison, Tessa Monina, Zoë Hughes; to my wonderful editor, Jane Struthers; to my utterly supportive agent, Bruce Hyman; to my dear family and friends; and to that infinitely intuitive and gifted artist, Helen Jones, for being my co-creator on a project that required both endurance and telepathic powers …

EDDISON • SADD EDITIONS

Project Editors....Tessa Monina and Zoë Hughes
Editor....Jane Struthers
Proofreader....Nikky Twyman
Creative Director....Nick Eddison
Senior Art Editor....Sarah Howerd
Mac Designer....Brazzle Atkins
Card Photography....Stephen Marwood
Production....Karyn Claridge and Charles James